Minding the Law

By the same author

In Love and War: the Lives of Sir Harry and Lady Smith
(co-written with David Rooney)

Scapegoats: Thirteen Victims of Military Injustice

Royal Betrayal: the Great Baccarat Scandal of 1890

The Lady of Kabul: Florentia Sale and the
Disastrous Retreat of 1842

Minding the Law

The *hazardous* and *hilarious* world of handling *complaints* against barristers

MICHAEL SCOTT

Marble Hill London

First published by Marble Hill Publishers in 2023

Flat 58 Macready House
75 Crawford Street
London W1H 5LP
www.marblehillpublishers.co.uk

A CIP catalogue record for this book is available from the British
Library.

ISBN: 9781739265700
Cover design by Paul Harpin
Printed and bound by Biddles Books

TABLE OF CONTENTS

ACKNOWLEDGEMENTS

Without Francis Bennett, this book would merely be a chapter in Tales for Tabitha – A Letter to my Granddaughter. Not only has he been my publisher but also mentor, editor and supportive friend. I am most grateful.

My beloved wife, Veronica, although self-proclaimed 'variously educated' has a rather better grip on grammar and syntax than what I have. I am indebted to her for the 'red ink corrections.'

Over my nine years working for the Bar, I was wonderfully looked after and protected by my inestimable PA, Anju. The Executive Secretaries, Jenny, Adrian and Oliver advised and held my hand and Freddie and Bhavna, our in-house solicitors, threw me a lifebelt when needed. All had tolerance and a well developed sense of humour, so essential in the world in which we operated.

I very much enjoyed working with the ladies and gentlemen of the Professional Conduct Committee, who not only freely gave up their time attending, and briefing at, long formal meetings but also provided me with essential Opinions when I floundered in the legal quagmire.

AUTHOR'S NOTE

For reasons of confidentiality, names have been redacted, less those in the public domain. As this is written up to 25 years after the events took place, "some recollections may vary" as Her Majesty the Queen is said to have remarked in a different context.

GLOSSARY

Every institution uses jargon as a shorthand and a way of saving time. However, you have to belong to the institution to know the words. For non-barristers, like me, I thought it useful to have a glossary for quick reference.

Adjudication Panel. Panel I chaired with a barrister and layman, dealing with Inadequate Professional Service.

Affidavit. An affidavit is a written statement from an individual which is sworn to be true. An affidavit is used along with witness statements to prove the truthfulness of a certain statement in court.

Amicus Curiae. Latin for 'friend of the court'. A non-party with an interest in the outcome of a pending lawsuit who argues or presents information in support of or against one of the parties to the lawsuit.

Back Sheet. A solicitor's formal instructions to a barrister.

Bar Council. Organisation responsible for running all aspects of the barristers' world.

Bencher. Senior barristers on the committees running their Inns.

BMIF. Bar Mutual Insurance Fund. All self-employed barristers are required by the Bar Council to purchase their professional indemnity insurance with Bar Mutual. It is an offence under the Code of Conduct not to do so.

BSB. Bar Standards Board. The organisation that took over the complaints system in 2006 on my departure.

Burden of Proof. In criminal cases, the burden of proof is on the prosecution, and the standard required of them is that they prove the case against the defendant beyond reasonable doubt. The standard of proof in civil cases is that of the balance of probabilities, which is rather less.

Cab Rank Rule. This rule made it mandatory for a qualified and available barrister to accept a case. It prevented 'cherry picking' attractive cases or avoiding the unpleasant ones.

Calderbank Offer. This is a settlement offer made on a 'without prejudice' except costs basis. The without prejudice rule will generally prevent statements made in a genuine attempt to settle an

1

existing dispute, whether made in writing or orally, from being put before the court as evidence of admissions against the interest of the party which made them.

Call. Date barrister called to the Bar ie started work.

CCRC. Criminal Cases Review Commission is the official independent body that investigates potential miscarriages of justice.

Chambers. An organisation to which a barrister belongs for administration.

A Civil Restraint Order (formerly called a Grepe v Loam order). This prevents the issue of further applications within a single set of proceedings without the permission of a nominated Judge and usually lasts for the duration of the proceedings. Any application made without permission is regarded as dismissed and the other party does not need to respond. The Court has stated that this order is appropriate when the claimant has shown an obsessive resort to litigation and made a number of applications in a single set of proceedings all of which have been dismissed for being totally without merit.

Clerks. Non-legally qualified clerks in chambers responsible for giving solicitors' instructions to barristers and arranging their fees.

Conditional Discharge. A discharge is a type of conviction where a court finds you guilty but does not give you a sentence because the offence is very minor. The conviction could be an absolute discharge or conditional, where the court could still impose a sentence if you break the conditions.

Consent Order. A consent order is a record of an agreement which has been reached. Once agreed, it is submitted to the court for approval. Once the order has been given court approval, it has legal force. The individual is bound by the order in the same way as if a decision had been imposed by the court. It can be used to consent to final issues alongside a divorce. Consent orders can cover a range of legal issues following separation and can be made at any time during a case, as long as it is before a case has come to a final determination.

Contempt of Court. Contempt of court, often referred to simply as "contempt", is the offence of being disobedient to or disrespect-

GLOSSARY

ful toward a court of law and its officers in the form of behaviour that opposes or defies the authority, justice, and dignity of the court.

Counsel. A barrister. QC – Queen's Counsel, a very senior barrister; now, of course, KC, King's Counsel.

CSA. The Child Support Agency's function was to calculate how much child maintenance was due, and the collection, enforcement and transferral of the payment from the non-resident parent to the person with care. For this to work, the CSA had to be requested by one of the parents; or to generate a recovery case, the parent with care had to be on Benefits. The CSA was abolished and replaced in 2012 by its successor, the Child Maintenance Service (CMS).

Disciplinary Tribunal. Highest range of disciplinary judgement.

Dunning-Kruger Effect. The Dunning-Kruger effect, in psychology, is a cognitive bias whereby people with limited knowledge or competence in a given intellectual or social domain greatly overestimate their own knowledge or competence in that domain relative to objective criteria or to the performance of their peers or of people in general.

Executive Secretary. Individuals who worked with me.

Extended Civil Restraint Order. This is an order against a person who has persistently issued claims or made applications which are totally without merit. It can last three years, but can be renewed for a further three. If the order is ignored, the person can be in contempt of court and may receive a prison sentence.

F & B. Further and Better (information required). Very often I had to correspond extensively with a complainant.

Form E. A Form E is a standard Statement which both parties will complete with a view to providing each other with a complete picture of their financial position.

GBH. Grievous Bodily Harm is a criminal offence under the Offences against the Person Act 1861. It is a more serious crime than Actual Bodily Harm - as committing GBH means causing extremely serious injuries which severely affect the health of the victim. These can include broken bones or permanent disfigurement.

GLOSSARY

In Camera. Latin for 'in a chamber'. Generally, in-camera describes court cases, parts of it, or process where the public and press are not allowed to observe the procedure.

Inns of Court. Lincoln's Inn, Middle Temple, Inner Temple and Gray's Inn. Institutions to which barristers belong.

IPS. Inadequate Professional Service. The lowest level of misdemeanour by a barrister, not amounting to misconduct.

Law Society. Equivalent of the Bar Council for solicitors. The professional association that represents solicitors.

Legal Aid Certificate. The Legal Aid Agency can issue a certificate which will set out the amount of money that can be spent on a case and the type of legal aid granted. The Agency will complain if this money is exceeded or misused.

Litigant in Person. A litigant in person is an individual, company or organisation that has rights of audience (this is, the right to address the court) and is not represented in a court of England and Wales by a solicitor or barrister.

LSO. Legal Services Ombudsman. He/she oversees the work of the Law Society and Bar Council. The LSO produces an annual report which is eagerly anticipated. The LSO has considerable powers of criticism, orders to re-examine a complaint and fining.

McKenzie Friend. A person who assists a litigant in person in a court of law by prompting, taking notes, and quietly giving advice. They need not be legally trained or have any professional legal qualifications. In the eyes of professionals, a beastly nuisance.

Opinion. Carefully written consideration by a barrister.

Part 36 Order. Part 36 is a provision in the Civil Procedure Rules designed to encourage parties to settle disputes without going to trial. If a party does not accept an offer made under Part 36 (a "Part 36 offer"), it risks being made liable to pay more in interest and/or costs on a judgment than if no offer had been made.

Part Heard. A matter is part heard when court proceedings have started but are adjourned to another date.

PCC. Professional Conduct and Complaints Committee.

Prima Facie. The Latin term prima facie means "at first glance," or "at first appearance," and it is generally used to describe how a situation appears on initial observation. In the legal system, prima facie is commonly used to refer to either a piece of evidence which is presumed to be true when first viewed, or a legal claim in which enough evidence is presented to support the validity of the claim.

Pro Bono (Publico). Pro bono work, literally 'for the public good' ie free, is legal advice or representation provided free of charge by legal professionals in the public interest. This can be to individuals, charities or community groups who cannot afford to pay for legal help and cannot get legal aid or any other means of funding.

Proceeds of Crime. This is the term given to money or assets gained by criminals during the course of their criminal activity. The authorities have powers to seek to confiscate these assets so that crime doesn't pay.

Secure Unit. A secure unit in prison is where extremely dangerous prisoners or violent psychiatric patients are kept.

Security of Costs. An order which requires a party (often the claimant) to pay money into court, or provide a bond or guarantee, as security for their opponent's costs of litigation.

Senior Partner. Head, or senior lawyer, of a solicitor's firm.

Silk. Queen's/King's Counsel. A superior barrister. See above.

Slip Rule. The court may at any time correct an accidental slip or omission in a judgment or order and a party may apply for a correction without notice. The sole purpose of the rule is to allow amendments to be made to judgments and orders that are the result of typographical errors or any accidental omissions: it does not give parties scope to attempt to insert any further clauses into a judgment and order that did not reflect the thinking and the intention of the court at the time the judgment and order were given. Any substantive mistake (i.e. a mistake of law) may only be rectified by way of appeal.

Sponsor. A member of the PCC dealing with a complaint.

SSAFA. Soldiers Sailors and Air Force Association. Armed Forces Charity. SSAFA Visitors provide support to isolated people living at home or in residential care. A friendly chat is an important aspect of the role but the Visitor must be able to recognise

GLOSSARY

any other support needed. They are worth their weight in gold.

Summary Hearing. Medium level disciplinary panel.

Tariff. A tariff is set which means the offender is given a specific number of years they have to serve in prison before they can be considered for release. The tariff is decided by a variety of factors including the seriousness of the crime. The Indeterminate Custodial Sentence can be used for the most serious sexual and violent offences, those which carry a penalty of 10 years or more, and can mean that the prisoner can, potentially, be imprisoned for life. Offenders serving sentences of between three months and four years, with certain exceptions for violent and sexual offenders, may also be eligible for release on a home detention curfew.

Vexatious Litigant. Vexatious litigants are individuals who persistently take legal action against others in cases without any merit, who are forbidden from starting civil cases in courts without permission. To stop a vexatious individual litigant issuing repeated applications, a party can apply for an Extended Civil Restraining Order against them.

Wasted Cost Application. This is an application against a legal representative whose conduct in proceedings has been shown to be "improper, unreasonable or negligent" to "show cause" why they should not be responsible for the costs incurred as a result of that conduct.

COMPLAINTS PROCESS

This is the flowchart I designed for my interview and how
the system worked.

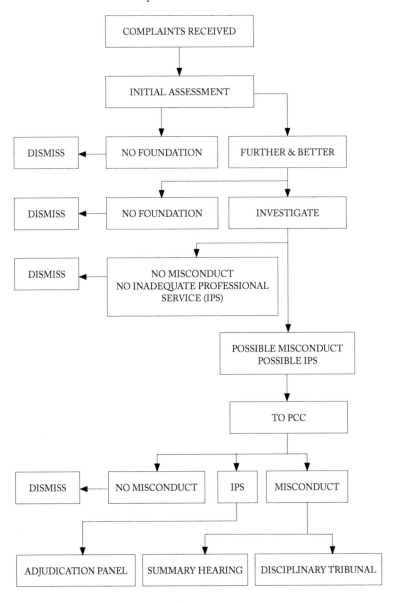

1
To the bar

IN THE FALL, AS AMERICANS charmingly call it, of 1996, I thought I ought to start looking for a job as I was to lose mine in March the following year. I was 55.

It is not an age when one is immediately attractive to head-hunters and moguls of industry. I had some 35 year's experience as an Army officer, had smelt high-explosive Semtex in Northern Ireland and the whiff of cordite in the Falklands but what good was this? The days of pipe-smoking Majors, in their leather-elbowed tweed jackets, bursars of minor Public Schools, were long gone. They had been replaced by people with degrees in economics, well versed in Health and Safety and employment legislation. Golf club Secretary? Much the same, anyway I didn't play golf. I had avoided budgets until the final years of my service, so the financial world would have been a mystery. Trade? Negotiations with their Unions? Hardly; coming from a hierarchical organisation where the nearest you got to shop floor representation was the euphemistically-called Battalion Welfare Committee, which usually concerned itself with the occasional incidence of wire wool in the chips and whether Jeans could be worn outside barracks. Working for a Charity? This was a possibility but I knew I did not have the skill or imagination to raise funds.

Too young, I thought, for the slippers and the pipe, and

letters to *The Times*. I didn't play Bridge, shoot or hunt. I had no yacht or mistress. I was no linguist unlike Charles V, Holy Roman Emperor, 1500–58, 'To God I speak Spanish, to women Italian, to men French, and to my horse - German'. Disgracefully, even after a number of years in Germany, I couldn't do much better than 'Noch ein bier und Bratwurst bitte.' Hopeless at tennis and no gardener, what was I to do? The arid desert of retirement loomed. At least I could have a gap year or, more probably, a gap month. I'd gone straight from school to Sandhurst and always envied my pre-university chums their spliff smoking and Gyppy tummy experiences in the Himalayas. Now was the chance; head for the hills with the rucksack.

I did, however, have one advantage. A few years previously I was a guinea pig in an Army experiment. This was not, in case you ask, some exposure to chemicals at Porton Down, but the Army had eventually reached the conclusion that while they did much in terms of re-settlement courses to find jobs for soldiers, they had neglected their senior officers. (Having said that, one enterprising friend of mine found a course on how to play the piano, paid for by Her Majesty. 'How did you swing that?' I asked. 'Simple,' he said, 'I told them I was seeking a job in a night club'). The Army contacted three Outplacement Agents. These were not head-hunters but career advisers to detect your worth and value, and help you to project that to a potential employer. Mine were Sanders and Sidney and my colleagues went to the other two. Depending on our reports, the Army would then select one firm to handle the retiring officers. Not unnaturally, I was given the five star treatment. I filled in copious forms about my background, likes and dislikes, what I thought I could do and, firmly, what I knew I could not do. I was subjected to mock interviews and consistently worked on a draft CV. Once I was asked, 'What qualities do you think you have to gain employment in the City?' Floored, I flippantly replied, 'Well, I know how far an 81 mm mortar fires.' 'Might be useful at Canary Wharf,' was the reply. I very much liked the staff and they gave me much confidence and a fireproof CV, in which I hardly recognised myself.

In those days, Friday's *Times* carried job advertisements in the back pages. I wrote off to a few, without much real hope, and was rewarded, sometimes with a nice letter, but more often with no response at all. One of my friends, who had secured a job, told me that he'd made countless applications. 'You need at least five replies before you are summoned for an interview,' he said. 'Then you'll probably go through another five interviews before you get a job, which will be well below your current salary'. All a bit depressing.

A predecessor but one in my final job in the Army as Military Secretary, was Lieutenant General Sir William Rous. He was a man of immense charm and style, dying much too early as the much loved Colonel of the Coldstream Guards. He had immensely high standards. He, however, found it incredibly difficult to find a job. I sometimes wondered whether his immaculate dark suit, stiff collar, pearl tie-pin and highly polished shoes didn't put potential employers off. Occasionally, he'd drop into my office to ask if I'd been approached by anyone looking for a senior former officer. Sadly, the answer was, invariably, no. Once, he'd been for an interview, I think, for the job of Chief Executive of the Automobile Association. 'How did it go?' I asked. 'Hopeless, Mike. And the lino was dirty.' Later I spotted an advertisement for the first Lay Commissioner of the Bar Council, specifically to deal with complaints against barristers. I thought this would suit Willie down to the ground, cut it out and sent it to him. For a man who replied to letters by return of post, he, uncharacteristically, made no response. I merely thought that it didn't attract him and let it lie. A few weeks later, I thought about it again and wondered whether I could do it? It seemed to me to be a procedure involving a non-legal, commonsense approach to problems; dealing with matters governed by strict rules; answering to a disciplinary committee and, from time to time, handling disappointed complainants and/or barristers. As Military Secretary, I was responsible for the promotion and appointments of officers. So there were distinct parallels; I operated under strict rules but fairness and compassion had a part to play when they needed adjusting;

TO THE BAR

I dealt personally with officers, disappointed they had not been promoted or secured the job they were after and I was well used to answering to the Army Board on future senior Generals' posts. Additionally, the Bar Council, rather like the Army was a Blue Chip organisation where discipline, in the best sense, mattered.

I asked my wonderful PA whether she'd kept an advertisement, I thought, something to do with lawyers? Yes, she had. So I looked at it again and sent off for the details. Back came a considerable amount of documentation, explaining exactly how the Bar saw the inadequacy of the present system (barristers, basically, dealing with complaints against other barristers) and how they saw the new system working under, importantly, a layman. I looked through it carefully and wrote a response. The Bar Council did not want a CV; they were carrying out their own recruitment without a head-hunter. My immaculate CV remained in its drawer.

To my surprise, I was summoned to an interview in the Boardroom of the Bar Council in Chancery Lane and given the names of those who would be interviewing me. These included the Chairman of the Bar, the Chief Executive, a lady lay representative and another barrister. A formidable group. I now took it extremely seriously, reading all the detail I'd been sent and trying to work out what was required and my approach. I was closely helped by my Military Assistant, Lieutenant Colonel Angus Loudon. Together, we worked out some 35 questions I could be asked and formulated the answers so that they'd come over with fluency in the interview. These ranged from 'General Scott, as a former senior officer, do think you can really work with all sorts and get your sleeves rolled up, when you, currently, even have someone to open your car door?'; to 'General Scott, I note you haven't been to University. How are you going to deal with very clever barristers?' Of course, neither of these were asked but it was as well to be armed. One thing I did put together was a flow-chart of what happens to a complaint when it arrives, to where it is finalised. I'd written this out on landscape orientated 'Word' but Angus corrected it by producing a much better version in portrait with the complaint arriving at the top of the sheet and finishing at the bottom.

The day before the interview, I arranged for Angus and his right-hand man to give me the real works. I'd never had an interview before and I wanted to be as fire-proof as possible. They sat behind the dining room table in my office and I sat on a chair in the middle of the room rather like the famous painting of the Cromwellians interviewing a small Royalist boy, 'When did you last see your father,' painted by William Yeames in 1878. Rightly, they pulled no punches and, while feeling mentally bruised, it gave me the confidence for the following day. I had also looked up the background on my interviewers. One, for instance, enjoyed skiing. So did I. Not that we were going to discuss skiing but it helped to place him.

The day came. Shoes not too highly polished, soft collared shirt and nondescript tie. I was driven to Chancery Lane in my staff car but dropped off some distance from the offices and my driver, the redoubtable Sgt Moir, parked well away. I had learned the lesson of a senior officer, coming out from his interview, for another job, saying to the Receptionist, 'Well, that went pretty well. Has my car arrived?' He didn't get the job. The arrangements were exactly how Angus and I had visualized; my interlocutors were arrayed one side of a large, highly polished table, and I the other. I don't really remember much of the detail; they were charming, non-aggressive and I warmed to them. Once I was asked what I knew of the Law. As the answer was zero, which, of course, was what they wanted, I tried some light-heartedness, and replied, 'Well, I know you can't park on a double yellow line.' Not a flicker, not even a smile. Ouch, I thought, I've bogged it. Anyway, I was determined to issue my flow-chart and handed out a copy to each of them. I apologised for it looking rather like a map for the London Underground. While there was little reaction, I sensed it had gone down well. There was no such diagram in their rules for dealing with complaints and I wondered whether some of them had actually seen a flow-chart like this.

I left, happy but certainly not for a moment thinking I'd

been successful. Sgt Moir asked how it had gone. I told him of my possible faux-pas of the yellow line. There was a small pause from a man who only just fitted into the car, having played in the second row of the scrum for the Royal Corps of Transport. He said, 'Don't worry. They are trained barristers, aren't they; used to disguising any surprise they might get in Court. Even if they thought it was funny, they are not going to say so'. An astute comment about a barrister's style which I was to encounter many times later.

A week later, I received a call from the Chief Executive offering me the job. I must have paused with shock as he said, 'Sorry, can you hear me?' I replied, 'Yes, I'm just picking myself off the floor'. A formal letter, he said, will follow. Will £60,000 do? Certainly (it was roughly what I was getting in the Army) – so the doom merchants were wrong. 'When are you leaving the Army?' '31st March,' I replied, not revealing my hope for a short spell of life under a large pack. 'Most grateful, then, if you could start on 1 April.' Bang goes my gap year. However, the bonus was, for the month of April, I had what was unattractively called Terminal Leave when I was paid for my first month out of the Army, presumably to find a job, and also paid by the Bar.

To my astonishment, and that of my friends, I'd got a job. Armed with *Bluff your way in Law*, I set off for a new life with the wigs and gowns.

2

Start Up

'WHAT DO WE CALL YOU?'

Morning of Day 1, sitting in my nice little office off Chancery Lane, having no real idea of what I was going to do, I was approached by the large, immaculate figure of a retired police Inspector on the Bar Council staff. I'd actually given it some thought. I was to mix with extremely senior barristers to the youngest, newly joined secretary, so one-fix-for-all was required. 'General?' Far too pompous and, anyway, my happy time in the Army was well behind me and nothing to do with the Secretariat. 'Commissioner?' Again grandiose and too distancing from the people with whom I'd be closely working. 'Mr Scott?' Awful.

'My family call me Mike except when they are cross with me, and then it's Michael. Will that do?' 'Yes,' he replied, clearly relieved to have that hurdle out of the way.

As the first Lay Commissioner, I was a bit of a novelty. The barristers, those who were mildly interested, wondered what I was going to make of it. The Chairman of the Bar, who had been instrumental in designing the new system, knew there were risks. The new complaints system was originally recommended in a report of the Standards Review Body chaired by Lord Alexander QC in 1994. After the inevitable working parties, consultation groups and temperature takings, the scheme was heavily defeated at a Bar Council meeting in November 1995. However, a ballot of the practising Bar, called as a result, ratified it by a margin of over 10%. Rules were amended to reflect a very closely fought and difficult compromise. 'Lions' and 'Dens' were words which came uncomfortably to mind.

In the Army, you tended to change your job every two to three years or so. As a young officer you'd progress through the junior ranks, perhaps becoming a mortar or anti-tank platoon commander or one of the battalion appointments such as adjutant (the commanding officer's chief executive) or the recce platoon commander, signals or intelligence officer. In all these, you got to know the 'ropes' on assuming the appointment from your predecessor and would be very ably helped by the nearest non-commissioned-officer. Later, you might go to a job on the Staff, away from your battalion. Again, you'd have a handover from the current incumbent – I once took over from an officer who later became a Field Marshal[1] - or attend a specialist course to equip you for the job. Not so, of course, with my employment as the first Complaints Commissioner; no one to take over from, no course to attend and with only a secretariat to advise. So, at age 56, I was taking up a completely new job; not one anyone had ever done before. I was starting with a clean sheet of paper. Of course, I can only guess why I was lucky enough to be selected. Maybe it was because while, as an Army officer, you gradually progress up through the ranks, you never really (or should not) lose touch with the soldiers who are doing the hard graft below you. Whereas in the commercial or, say, diplomatic world, board members or ambassadors become inevitably distanced from the workers. So, I'd have a certain amount of empathy with shop-floor complainants or barristers at the bottom rungs of the ladder. Or it may simply have been that the selectors realised I'd seen some of the rougher edges of life and humanity and therefore might have a thick enough skin to handle difficult complainants or, indeed,

---

1. Field Marshal the Lord Guthrie of Craigiebank, GCB, GCVO, OBE, DL.

barristers. I'd had a certain amount of background in dealing with problems with a degree of fairness and understanding. Anyway, it was a challenge which I was keen to face.

The problem with self-regulation, which was, effectively, what the Bar was doing, was that many of the aggrieved believed, when they were unsuccessful with their complaint, it was because of the inbuilt bias against them. With my eventual experience, however, practitioner involvement meant that it was harder for a professional to pull the wool over the eyes of a disciplinary body. Conversely, lay people made a vital contribution to professional bodies, having a clearer and more informed view about what the rules themselves should say. In essence, it was more user-friendly, more flexible and less costly than one run by the Government or the courts.

What was new?

I was appointed the first Lay Complaints Commissioner to oversee the complaints handling process and refer to the Professional Conduct and Complaints Committee (PCC) any complaint where I thought a barrister might have been at fault. I was also to advise the Committee about matters of inadequate professional service. The creation of the new concept of 'inadequate professional service' (IPS) was defined as 'such conduct towards the lay client or performance of professional services for the lay client which fall significantly short of that which is to be reasonably expected of a barrister in all the circumstances'. It was not professional misconduct; Summary Hearings and Disciplinary Tribunals had the powers of punishment for that as decided by the PCC. The Adjudication Panel was to award redress of various kinds in cases involving IPS.

I had considerable authority. Primarily, I was to oversee the way in which complaints were handled. I had a staff of three Executive Secretaries, who were supported by their own secretaries. I could conciliate between client and barrister where appropriate. I was to dismiss complaints which were clearly without merit. I attended PCC meetings to explain why I'd referred a case to them. I chaired Adjudication Panels investigating matters of IPS. Finally,

START UP

I recruited Lay Representatives to attend the various disciplinary bodies of the Bar Council. Totally different to my previous life, I had a lot to learn in a short time. People used to ask, kindly, how I was coping in civilian life – no limo to pick me up in the morning, for instance. Actually, I found it very unstressful; I commuted for 20 minutes on the Central Line, buried in my *Spectator*, which lasted a week, then welcomed at the office block by the security guard and, upstairs, the pretty secretaries.

The Code of Conduct of the Bar of England and Wales (note; not Scotland or Northern Ireland) was a seriously heavy-weight tome which made the Manual of Military Law look like something you'd find for light reading in the downstairs loo. There were penalties ranging from permanent disbarring to a rap over the knuckles for failing to answer a communication from the Bar Council (or me) within three weeks. Of course, I didn't have to take it all in but know where to find things particularly relevant to what I was doing. Initially, my hand was held by the Executive Secretaries.

IPS seemed to be the major element of disquiet among the Bar. It was designed to cover breaches of the Code which might not be considered serious enough to merit the stigma of a finding of professional misconduct. Examples might include delay, rudeness, late attendance at court and others which caused worry and inconvenience to the lay client. It did not cover negligence, which was a matter of misconduct; neither did it cover what a barrister actually did in court. Lay complainants found the latter very difficult to understand. Later, I tried to explain to barristers that what he/she did in court was a matter for the legal process and in the hands of the judge. Remedies for IPS ranged from a formal apology from the barrister to the lay client, reduction in fees and compensation up to £2,000. The latter proved equally difficult for barristers. When I started, compensation could only be levied if the lay client had suffered loss recoverable at law. This meant, for instance, if your barrister was late and you had to make, say, a later, higher priced, train journey, you could only recover the cost of the ticket, not a sum for being mucked about. Eventually,

I managed to have this changed but not before being put in my place by a very senior, and charming, Silk who explained to me what the legal definition of compensation was. His view was that you couldn't be compensated for something you hadn't legally lost. Mine was that you should have a chunk of money for being buggered about by an idle barrister. I won.

Chairing the Adjudication Panel into IPS was interesting because, in a sense, I was dealing with human, non-legal failings by a barrister. It would take place in my office at 5pm, when Court work had finished. I was assisted by a barrister and lay representative from the PCC. The 'accused' was not present. We would agree the finding and my PA would type it onto the computer at the time. I refused to have minutes circulated later to the attendees with all the nitpicking over words and waste of time that that can produce. We made the decision there and then and it was transmitted to the complainant and barrister first thing the following day.

There were some very senior barristers who told me, much later, quite candidly that they had opposed the scheme but were now relieved that it had worked. I could understand their worries. This was something totally new being orchestrated by a former soldier from a world about which they knew nothing. One was absolutely fascinated how we soldiers lived on operations. Probably never having slept a night anywhere apart from a bed, he simply couldn't grasp what it was like to be tired, wet, cold and hungry, trying to get some rest in a sodden sleeping-bag. When I revealed that, in the Falklands, I hadn't taken my clothes off for 14 days, I could see the horror on his face.

Of course, interest in the new procedure was not confined to members of the Bar. The legal Press and the National Consumer Council questioned it. In January 1997 (I did not assume the appointment until April) Robert Owen QC, Chairman of the Bar, who had taken over from Peter Goldsmith QC, who appears later in this story, held a Press Conference, with me sitting at his right hand, firmly close-lipped. He explained the IPS scheme and how it had been watered down to reflect the concerns of the criminal bar that it would prompt complaints from every convicted client. The Commissioner, he argued, would be very vigorous in filtering complaints – at present about 70% were without foundation. I enjoyed the confidence he had in me, yet totally unproven.

Overseeing the work of the Bar Council and the Law Society was the Legal Services Ombudsman (LSO). In England and Wales, the LSO was a statutory officer who investigated allegations about the improper, ineffective or inefficient way that complaints about lawyers are handled by their respective self-regulating professional bodies (us). The Ombudsman was appointed by, and was answerable to, the Lord Chancellor and Secretary of State for Justice. The post was abolished under the Legal Services Act 2007, which was after I'd left. The Ombudsman could:

- Recommend or order that the professional body re-investigate a complaint;
- Formally criticise the professional body;
- Award compensation for distress or inconvenience to the complainant.

There were three LSOs during my time but for my last six years she was Zahida Manzoor. The bulk of her work was dealing with the solicitors' complaints body. The Law Society came in for some pretty severe criticism for their complaint handling. This was not surprising as there were many more of them than barristers and they were the first people the client dealt with. Solicitors also handled client's money and the barristers' fees, so there was always scope for a financial argument.

It was important to have a good relationship with the LSO and, I think, on the whole it worked. She was supported by a legal team but much less of the quality I had at my disposal in the PCC where I had some of the top Silks in the Country. This occasionally led to legal argument when I had to deploy the might of my team from the PCC. We had an annual conference and, on one occasion, I vividly remember our team travelling by train (First Class, of course) to the LSO's office in Manchester, led by the Chairman of the PCC, later a High Court Judge. Gazing out of the window of our comfortable compartment, I remarked how lovely the rolling fields of corn looked. Our leader said, 'Yes, Mike but more Corot than Matisse, I think. Corot executed some 300 paintings in his time; 350 of which are in America'.[2]

But enough of the technicalities, how was I going to fill my day? I relied on my very experienced Executive Secretaries. One, a former Wren Lieutenant Commander could be <u>so</u> icily polite on the telephone that it was totally disarming. We had a small office of in-house qualified solicitors, with a well developed sense of humour, one of whom asked, when I told her we were going to *Parsifal* that night, whether it was from Gatwick or Stansted. I had a wonderful Personal Assistant who kept the drawbridge firmly secured against the barbarians – complainants *and* barristers. My telephone extension number was 1348, so, naturally, when I was occasionally allowed to answer it myself, I responded 'Black Death'. Just outside my office was the Receptionist at her desk and, with my door open, I could hear her dealing with people. Senior moguls of office life often forget that a Receptionist, who is paid comparatively little, is vital, being the first voice an outsider hears. If the Receptionist is intolerant, badly spoken or unintelligible (to say nothing of '*Your call is important to us. I'll put you on hold....'Vivaldi music*), it reflects badly on the system. We were blessed with ours, who was charming and normally robust, but one day, I heard her reduced to tears by a caller. I leapt out of my chair, seized her telephone and gave the miscreant a bit of the barrack room vernacular. He didn't ring again. We were blessed with a group of secretaries who did the real hard work of typing and filing. Their highlight of the year was the fire practice. We all had to leave the building and congregate at points outside to be counted and generally hang around. This was bliss for the secretaries to get away from their desks and hobnob with the hunky firemen.

Another joy was the Postroom. Our world, and that of the barristers, was then run mainly on paper; the world of emails and texts was still in its infancy. WhatsApp, Facebook, Instagram and

2. He was wrong. Corot painted a staggering 3,000 in his lifetime.

START UP

Twitter hadn't been, thankfully, invented. The distribution and collection of vast quantities of Opinions, files, letters and memoranda was operated by clerks from barristers' chambers and our stalwart men of the Postroom. Their trolleys trundled ceaselessly round the Inns and chambers of the Chancery Lane world. About four of them; their lair was in the basement of the Bar Council offices. They were commanded by a senior personage (in my previous life, probably the rank of Sergeant) for whom political correctness was unknown. It was a smoke-filled dungeon, fuelled by hot sweet tea, banter and ribaldry. Occasionally, when in need of respite from the arcane world of legal argument, I would descend to their empire for light hearted anecdotes and naughty stories, taking me back to my life with soldiers. Indeed, one of them had been a Lance Bombardier in the Royal Artillery. Predictably, it took him two years before he could stoop to calling me 'Mike'. They were also responsible for low level administration; wiring plugs, changing light bulbs, oiling locks and easing drawers; that sort of thing but only, to their infuriation and frustration, after sanction by the Human Resources operative in the Office. Even we had become victims of the Health and Safety secret police. One of the bulbs embedded in the ceiling of my office blew and I asked my PA to have the boys replace it. 'No', she said, regretfully, 'I have to report it to Human Resources'. Three days went by and nothing had happened. 'Get a bulb with petty cash when you next go out for a sandwich and I'll do it,' I told her. Bulb appeared; I stood on my desk and replaced it. A day later two of the Postroom boys appeared with a ladder and a bulb. I told them, with a certain amount of glee and self-satisfaction what I'd done. Withdrawal of helpers amidst much hilarity and cries of 'You're very naughty. We'll have to report you to HR.' A final brush with the HR lady came when she inspected my office for fire regulations. I'm one of those rather pathetic something-retentive people that likes a clutter free desk, so I had a small table adjacent to the desk on which were the In and Out trays. 'Oh, you can't have that. There's no room for you to exit the office on 'FIRE', she said. I told her if there was a fire, I'd be over my desk and through the door before she could say, 'Knife.' Not the point – so she spent the next ten minutes rearranging my furniture. The moment she left I put it back to where it had been, to the general satisfaction of the watching secretaries. HR was not seen in the land again.

I needed, quickly, to absorb the 'feel' of an organisation about which I knew virtually nothing. I knew, personally, only two barristers; one was a Silk earning vast amounts of money in Hong Kong (he even drove Rolls Royce, which could hardly have progressed from third gear, in a land where 'face' was everything) and the other a specialist in maritime law which, over my subsequent nine years, I received not one single complaint. I started with chambers in the Chancery Lane vicinity, trying to familiarise myself with all the various areas of practice - criminal, matrimonial, employment, medical negligence, defamation, human rights, financial, intellectual property and so on. I then went out to the Circuits and called, later, on the Leaders of the various Associations. Throughout, I was warmly welcomed, given time and answers to what must have seemed to most of the barristers thoroughly naïve and ignorant questions. I remember asking one very senior criminal Silk on the Northern Circuit how he coped, defending some of the most repellent in the Land. 'Yes, Mike, difficult, but what you must be quite clear on is that everyone is entitled to the best defence they can get'. Here was a man who ran a daily gauntlet of screaming women when going into court to defend a nurse accused of multiple baby killing. He admitted his palms were raw from digging his nails into his hand to overcome emotion.

The way I saw it, I was no pussy-cat for the barristers and the complainants needed to realise that. I took no sides. I wanted the complainants to understand, in, often, layman's language, what had gone wrong and whether the barrister had erred or done the best he could under the circumstances. At the same time, I was not to be perceived, by the Bar, as some do-gooder for the man in the street. I realised only too well what a successful complaint against a barrister could do for their career.

Did it work?

3

Pooh Traps for the Profession

"Now then
This is an interesting situation
my mate got a young son in jail. A Junior offenders
institute. his dad had words
off solicitor to say
if yer can find 16,000
cash. I no sumBody in
Power position, oo will get
im out of jail. But a court
hearing came along and
and the son went Bac to
Jail. dad is in a Fercin
Temper. olavim shot ses im.
Barsterd tooc our Fercin
muny".
(Signed by the writer, with his address)

23

MINDING THE LAW

IAGREED WITH THE WRITER that, indeed, it was an interesting situation but one for the Complaints Commissioner? How did I go about my business?

With a first look at a complaint, very often, such as this one, I needed more information from the complainant; what in the jargon is called 'Further and Better'. This could result in an extensive exchange of letters. Sometimes, it would irritate the complainant who wanted a swift triumphal end and, to others, it produced a cathartic release in finding someone to whom they could unravel their woes. If I thought there was no case at all against the barrister, often to the fury or, at least, disappointment of the complainant, I'd dismiss the complaint. As a non-lawyer, of course, I needed help, from time to time, over legal problems.

The 'help' came from the high quality, five star organisation called the Professional Conduct and Complaints Committee (PCC). Of the many Committees, it was the premier one to be on if you had aspirations to further your career in the Bar Council. The PCC consisted of some 48 barristers, half of whom were QCs (Silks), and from a range of 'Call,' in other words from senior to relatively junior and, of course, an even gender split. They all had individual main areas of practice:

Criminal, Construction, Professional Negligence, Consumer Law, Chancery, Medical Negligence, General Commercial, Banking, Financial Services, Securities Markets, Insurance, Personal Injury, Employment Law, Industrial Tribunals, Licensing, Housing, Judicial Review, European Appeals, Extradition, Serious Fraud, Family Law, Defamation, Insolvency, Landlord & Tenant, Rights of Way, Intellectual Property, Tax Law.

This seemed to cover most things. However, it was not always that simple. Crime covered murder, robbery, grievous bodily harm, all sorts of sex, drugs, arson, fraud and motoring. There were straight complaints by solicitors against barristers, usually concealing fee disputes. Some complaints were purely political; a few barristers being politicians. Very occasionally there was barrister v. barrister. Finally, I was victim of some very direct personal complaints.

If I decided to investigate the complaint, my standard procedure was to send it to the barrister and their instructing solicitor for comment. Under the draconian Code of Conduct, the barrister was obliged to respond but not so solicitors. On the whole the latter would, and their contribution was valuable; reading between the lines one would get a very good feel of whether the barrister had erred or not. The solicitors who championed their barrister were worth their weight. However, there were others who were idle, slack and indifferent; the bottom of the pile. After waiting for what was an important part of my investigation in vain, I would write to the Senior Partner of the solicitors' firm, explaining that I was merely a seeker after truth and his firm's failure to reply would, surely, in due course, come to the notice of the Legal Services Ombudsman. Occasionally this had an electrifying effect, sometimes just rudeness.

If I felt there was something in it, I'd refer it to the PCC, through a 'sponsor' member who would write a brief for the Committee. (I once asked one of my favourite senior QC sponsors what he would charge for an Opinion on the amount of (free) work he had done for me on a very long complaint. He responded: 12 hours @ £250 an hour = £3,000). The Committee met once a fortnight with half the members and three or four lay representatives. It would have been fairly natural to label the two halves, Team One and Team Two, or Group A or B. However, this was seen to be discriminatory against the Twos and Bs. No one likes to be in the 2nd XI. What to do? A bright spark (not a barrister) suggested calling the two teams Scylla and Charybdis. As everyone knows, these were two immortal and irresistible monsters who bestrode the narrows of the Straits of Messina, destroying ships as they attempted to navigate through the stormy waters; just the job for people dealing with naughty barristers. While I'm on 2nd XIs, there is a story of a battalion of the Coldstream Guards camped, in the Canal Zone many years ago, next to a battalion of the Royal Australian Regiment. They got on extremely well and, one day, a couple of officers from each Regiment were walking past the Coldstream camp, outside which was a large Battalion sign with, underneath, their motto 'Nulli Secundus.' 'What's that mean?' the Australian asked. 'Second to None' the Coldstreamer proudly replied. A few days later, the same two walked past the Australian camp outside which was a large notice saying, 'None.'

The committee meetings were not for the faint hearted. The fate of the barrister rested in their hands where they could refer him/her to a Disciplinary Tribunal (effectively a Court Martial in my previous existence), a Summary Hearing (not so powerful) or an Adjudication Panel, which I chaired, dealing with Inadequate Professional Service. They could, of course, dismiss the complaint but only with the agreement of the lay represent- atives. Apart from the Adjudication Panel, once the complaint was considered by the PCC, it left my hands. Very occasionally I'd attend a Disciplinary Tribunal but merely as a spectator. I had no role to play.

Not all barristers were, understandably, fans of the new system, particularly if they'd had brushes with the disciplinary element.

Marc Beaumont, a barrister with Chambers in Windsor, became a champion of the barrister facing disciplinary proceedings under the regime of the new Bar Standards Board. In his 2020 book '*Beaumont on Barristers – A Guide to Defending Disciplinary Proceedings*'. Beaumont alleges, in some detail, what he calls the effective collapse of the Bar's system of discipline. Since 2006, there has been, he claims, "an unprecedented growth in litigation involving the BSB". The general decay in the process, he says, led to the creation of the Bar Tribunals and Adjudication Service from 2014. Of particular interest to me was his comment, in Chapter 1, on the pre-BSB system. 'Understanding, capturing, defining and explaining something unpleasant can be difficult. Underlying the regulation of barristers until the advent of the BSB in 2006, was a somewhat confused, barrister-driven interpretation of a post-Victorian and pseudo-public school attitude, manifesting itself as stigma attaching to the mere making of an allegation of professional misconduct. That attitude surfaced in the way in which the old PCC, which for years vested tremendous investigatory power in a retired NCO, treated barristers accused of professional misconduct. It was also revealed by the way in which the tribunals processed cases. This was on occasion carried out in an environment that was certainly as, if not, more, tensile and unpleasant, than any courtroom.' Not sure I appreciated being called a 'retired Non Commissioned Officer', however, his email, dated 26 May 2006, to Mark Stobbs, Head of Professional Standards after my retirement is in curious contrast. 'I hope he [my successor] has Mike's sense of the absurd and knows how to deal robustly with silly complaints. That requires a sense of humour. Mike saw men die for their country. That made some of the attacks on barristers seem pathetic in the general scheme of things. We may not fully appreciate Mike until he is gone'.

How did I do in my first year? There was, not unnaturally, considerable interest from the Bar Council, which had invested a good deal of faith in the new system. There were those who predicted failure. The general public couldn't care less, unless it directly affected them. The Government, in the shape of the Lord Chancellor, was indifferent unless the inadequacy of the Law Society and the Bar Council over complaints merited heavy interference. The Legal Press, whose journalists, of course, made their money by writing about such things, were much more interested. Indeed, before presenting my annual report to the Bar Council, I held a press conference. Rightly, the Council wanted to demonstrate what a good set up they had initiated and it was quite proper to have me explain that to the world. However, I did not find Press Conferences comfortable and had to work on my self-confidence. When a very junior officer in the Army, I'd been made the Battalion PR officer, mainly because (a) no one really knew what it stood for or entailed and (b), if they did, they didn't want to do it. In Kenya in 1962, our Sergeants' Mess had been given two lion cubs. They were looked after, in his married quarter, by the Pioneer Sergeant, Sgt Ryves, who built a compound for them in his back garden. The local Daily Express journalist thought this would be good copy – he was right – and interviewed Ryves in his quarter with the cubs paddling about. I was, as the PR officer, ordered to attend. I thought it all went pretty well with

Ryves warming to his theme that when we returned to London we'd have the lions parading with the Queen's Guard at Buckingham Palace and he was quite sure Prince Philip would approve. However, our stuffy senior officers in London had a different view. 'Regiment being brought into disrepute' or similar words were coming over the long distance telephone wires. Luckily for me, the Commanding Officer loved his lions, which went on to star in the movie *Born Free* and, of course, didn't come to London with us. He also disliked his pompous seniors in London and was far enough away not to have to take them too seriously. However, it was a lesson for me, at an early age, to be very careful with journalists.

The Legal Press were, on the whole, benign, and were not after my or the Bar Council's blood. They simply wanted to find out how it was going and detect any nonsense. I was, though, sensitive to the thought that they and the Consumer organisations might suspect the Bar merely 'doing what they did yesterday' under a different guise. After all I was a classic white, middle-aged man, ex-public school and a former Guards officer. One of them? So my first Annual Report, on which they based much of their comment, was important. Failure of the new system, which had taken time, energy and not without difficulty to establish, was not an option. I wrote this in the Introduction:

Aim. My aim has been to establish a fair deal for the complainant and the barrister. I have tried to give complainants the confidence that they will obtain proper consideration and their complaints will not be handled solely by barristers, yet, at the same time protect the barrister from frivolous and inappropriate allegations. I have valued my independence from the Bar, and while I am responsible, with the Bar Council's Head of Professional Standards and Legal Services, to the Chairman of the Bar for the efficient running of the system, the Council plays no part in my day-to-day decisions. This is extremely important in my dealings with lay clients and that independence is crucial to my activities.

POOH TRAPS FOR THE PROFESSION

My freedom of action has been critical. I have been able to ask potential witnesses for evidence, solicitors for statements and members of the PCC for advice on legal matters, without constraint. On occasions I have interviewed a complainant. I have been able to liaise with Leaders of Circuits, Chambers, Senior Clerks and Listing Officers. Contact with the Legal Services Ombudsman (LSO), the Ombudsman Association, Office for the Supervision of Solicitors and other organisations such as the National Consumer Council and Victim Support has been very helpful. I look forward to continuing such communication. I see it as essential in responding to the concerns of the public.

The leader of the journalists' pack was, undoubtedly, Joshua Rozenberg. In my time, he was the legal correspondent of *The Daily Telegraph*. He had qualified as a solicitor in 1976 and started in journalism at the BBC where he worked as a producer, reporter and then legal correspondent. He holds honorary doctorates in law from no less than four Universities and is an honorary Bencher of Gray's Inn. He won the Bar Council's Legal Reporting Award four times. In 2016, he was made an honorary QC. He is also a fellow member of the Garrick Club, which is even more important. I very much enjoyed his attendance at my press conferences. He told me that he remembered me more for my battered brief case which, since my 21st birthday had accompanied me round the world, than anything else. Once I buttonholed him afterwards for asking a sharp question and he said, 'Come on, Mike, I'm a journalist. That's what I do'. I was very honoured to have him write a Foreword to my book *'Royal Betrayal – The Great Baccarat Scandal of 1890[3].'* I'm sure his contribution resulted in the subsequent purchase of the film rights.

A close rival was Frances Gibb. Frances claimed Joshua's job was different in that he was in the broadcast media and she was, at heart, a journalist writing about the law. She saw Joshua

3. Endeavour Press, London 2017.

as a lawyer engaged in journalism. A neat distinction: she was appointed Legal Correspondent of *The Times* in 1982, at the age of thirty-one. As the first person to hold the post from outside the legal profession, she had to overcome some resistance from the then editor, Charles Douglas-Home, but persuaded him that journalistic independence and an ability to communicate to the public were more important. How right she was. She became Legal Editor of *The Times* in 2000. As Legal Correspondent and subsequently Legal Editor, Frances was in charge of daily reporting on legal news, as well as weekly pages on the law. In 2000, she established *The Times*' weekly *Law* supplement, the only legal pull-out to be published by a national newspaper in the UK. She served under nine editors on *The Times*, including William Rees-Mogg and John Witherow. After my first press Conference, she wrote:[4]

'Last weekend Mr Scott, a former major general, presented his first annual report to the Bar Council. He said in his report: "Any profession has its weak links and the Bar is no exception; a very small percentage of barristers are disciplined as a result of a criminal conviction. A slightly larger percentage makes mistakes through incompetence or cutting corners. Overwork or laziness leads to mishaps. Arrogance and self-importance result in rudeness and bombast. Sometimes, these can cause real disadvantage or distress to the complainants.'

There is plenty of scope for improvement. Above all, Mr Scott wants to get rid of the restrictions on when he can award up to £2,000 compensation for shoddy work. Strong opposition to the complaints system, particularly from the Criminal Bar, led to the rule that means people can be compensated only if they have suffered a financial loss which would be recoverable in the courts. But many people suffer distress or inconvenience which cannot be quantified, Mr

4. *The Times* 19 May 1998.

Scott says, and he should be able to award compensation for that.

He would also like more explanation given to people about the Bar's immunity from being sued for negligence – an immunity which consumer groups and others now argue should go. It means they cannot be sued over their work in court. And finally, he says, barristers can do more to avoid complaints in the first place. "The last thing I wish to do as a layman is to patronise barristers. But people going into court with no experience of court or lawyers can be very intimidated. Perhaps some of the younger ones who have battled their way to becoming a barrister could be quite pleased with themselves and a bit short with someone who has not the same grey cells as they have."

The Bar, he says, must remember the importance of client care and the need to treat clients as one would wish to be treated by a fellow professional.'

Writing more generally about lawyers' watchdogs, among which she included me:[5]

'The way the legal profession handles complaints about itself from the public is something of a running sore. Its history of dealing with them is littered with casualties and criticisms. In recent months though, both the Bar and Law Society have made a fresh stab at improving the service. The Bar has appointed its first Complaints Commissioner, Michael Scott, to head a new complaints system directed at the public rather than being just an internal disciplinary procedure.

The Bar standards review report, under Lord Alexander of Weedon, QC, said the immunity rule was "obscure" to lay clients and would appear that "lawyers were raising technical legal defences to protect themselves by a form of special pleading." He cautions the Bar against being too restrictive in its approach to the new powers. With both the Bar and

5. *The Times* 24 June 1997.

Law Society, critics are closely watching the way they handle complaints, one of the last areas of self-regulation. For the first time in years, there is hope of improvement. But if it turns out to be misplaced, "the pressures for a major shake-up of the system are likely to become irresistible."'

Grania Langdon-Down then wrote for *The Independent*.[6] Currently, she is a freelance legal journalist, having been a Press Association crime and legal affairs correspondent. Her piece had the title 'Why do barristers fear this man?' with a half page photograph of me. I wasn't sure whether to be flattered or worried that I might therefore become a target of some aggrieved barrister. My old friends thought it was a joke. She wrote:

'Very few letters of thanks cross the desk of General Michael Scott, the lay commissioner responsible for handling complaints against barristers. He is more likely to become the target of complainants who transfer their wrath from the barrister they are convinced wronged them, to Scott, when he dismisses their complaint.

One prisoner, however, took a more sanguine view. After hearing his complaint had been dismissed, the prisoner wrote to Scott: "I have even noticed you wrote to me in my language in order to help me understand easier. Keep up the good work. Thanks. PS I will win."

Many of the complaints arose from misunderstandings about a barrister's role and duties to the court and legal aid fund. But, of the 40 per cent of cases Scott referred to the PCC, about half were found to involve *prima facie* evidence of misconduct or inadequate professional service.

But Scott is keen to put his criticisms in perspective. "There are 9,400 barristers practising at the independent Bar. If each do on average 100 things a year that could be complained about, such as writing an opinion or representing someone in court, that represents one complaint per 1,700 actions.

6. *The Independent* 26 June 1998.

POOH TRAPS FOR THE PROFESSION

The poor old barrister is an easy target at the moment with talk of 'fat cats'.[7]

What the public doesn't realise is how difficult it is to become a barrister; how little you are paid at the bottom of the profession, and how much good work is done."

Not everyone is so enthusiastic about the Bar's self-regulatory procedures. Earlier this month, the Fabian Society called for the Bar to be stripped of its complaint handling powers and replaced by an independent body along the lines of the General Medical Council. Chris Swinson, the new head of the Institute of Chartered Accountants, has proposed that there be an independent body to oversee all self-regulated professions.

But Scott defended the current system. "I don't feel I am the last bastion between the Bar and central regulation. I think the Bar has got it right by recognising that unless they introduced a strong lay element, they could be vulnerable. I think they are ahead of the game."

One ongoing criticism of the Bar's complaint system is that it focuses too heavily on whether the barrister is right or wrong, rather than the effect on the complainant. Marlene Winfield, senior policy adviser for legal services for the National Consumer Council, echoed that point. "He has done well to get the complaints system up and running but he is doing it with one hand behind his back, as he himself admits. The combination of an extremely high standard of proof, the fact that in order to get compensation you have to show actual loss, and the immunity barristers have for their performance in court, is not really in the spirit of a proper complaints procedure."

However, Scott is under no illusions about what a complaint can mean to a barrister. "It can mean you will never make QC or judge, or solicitors might not instruct you. If you are suspended, that is your livelihood gone. What if it is not justified?"

Veronica Cowan is a freelance feature writer, contributing to many legal journals. In *The Lawyer*, she head-

7. Described by Roderic Wood QC, before he became a High Court Judge, as "Felines of the Fuller Figure."

ed an article 'Great Scott? Not quite, but showing promise'.[8]
A rather easy link to the Antarctic explorer (no relation) but
which, embarrassingly, appeared in my Wikipedia entry. I hasten
to say not placed by me. She wrote:

'The former major general will find his diplomatic skills
useful with a profession slow to note the need for an independent adjudicator. But despite seeing his "softly-softly"
tactics as appropriate, does he think the public perceive him as
being independent of the Bar? Scott concedes that complainants sometimes accuse him of being one of "them" – although
most ombudsmen suffer that label. In his first year, Scott received 532 complaints – an increase on previous years. The
main areas of dispute concern matrimonial, neighbourhood
and prisoners' disputes. He agrees that having a complaints
system probably encourages people to complain but says no
complaints could mean a public with little faith in the system.
Scott also believes the system must be open and advertise itself. Minority of barristers have resisted this, but he observes
that there is little point in having a complaints commissioner
that nobody knows about.

Roy Amlot QC, chairman of the Criminal Bar Association, says Scott is doing a very good job. There were reser-
vations before Scott's appointment, because of a fear that dis-
gruntled clients would jump on the bandwagon and misuse
the system as part of their appeals. This fear has been allayed
by his careful approach to investigations – he has proven good
at sifting the frivolous cases from those of genuine concern.

After a year in office, Scott's report card has an air of
caution. And the man who describes himself as "just a simple
soldier" may yet find complaints resolution to be a minefield'.

One of the areas which I thought important was the edu-
cation of barristers on the subject of how to avoid my clutches. I
was asked to lecture to Inns, usually after one of their Dining In
nights; once even between courses. I described myself as the sor-

8. *The Lawyer* 9 June 1998.

bet, cleaning the palate between courses. Either they didn't think it funny or were too young to know that that used to happen years ago. I very much enjoyed talking to aspiring barristers on Bar Vocational Courses. Faced with people who were young enough to be my children and as a complete non-lawyer, I happily warmed to my theme. An early scene in *The Raiders of the Lost Ark* came to mind when Indiana Jones faced a student who expressed her admiration by writing the word "LOVE" on her right eyelid and "YOU" on her left. Sadly it didn't happen to me but I was asked one question by an enterprising chap at the back, at Nottingham University, 'How much do you get paid and when do you finish your job?' I took it as a compliment but it might have been the reverse.

Another very good outlet was being invited to write an article, from time to time, for *Counsel*, the journal of the Bar of England and Wales. This was a well produced magazine, with a wide circulation among barristers. I wrote my first in August 1998, a year and a bit after I started, so important to get my 'lessons' across at an early stage. I called it:

Pooh Traps for the Profession.[9]

"Pooh rubbed his nose with his paw, and said that the Heffalump might be walking along, humming a little song, and looking up at the sky, wondering if it would rain, and so he wouldn't see the Very Deep Pit until he was half-way down, when it would be too late."

Poor communication is the cause of many complaints. We think we are so good at communicating – satellites, mobiles, internet, e-mail, teletex, ceefax,[10] but those of us who have been married for more than five minutes, soon realise that we are not.

In dealings with a lay client, what is straightforward, everyday bread and butter to the barrister, is loaded with stress, anxiety

9. *Winnie the Pooh – Chapter 5 Piglet meets a Heffalump* – A.A.Milne.
10. Don't forget this was 1998; the scourge of Twitter, Instagram and WhatsApp had yet to arrive.

and fear to the ordinary person. Relate it to the worry one might feel on going to see a medical consultant, having been referred by one's GP, for something possibly sinister, and one has probably got the level right. No one goes to a barrister for fun.

So, try to explain why you have turned up and not counsel I was expecting and with whom I had built up a rapport. I do not know what 'part heard' means. Although you only received the papers last night, you read them into the small hours, know all the detail and are fully on the ball. What the odds are and why they have changed (for the worse) since you gave me your rather more optimistic opinion a few months ago? Some skeletons, perhaps, have emerged from their cupboards, or your instructing solicitors have discovered some bad news. Why you did not call such and such a witness, or ask the numerous questions I told you to? Tell me the effect that some witnesses, or their responses to questions, have on a judge or jury. You also have to think quickly on your feet and, if a witness has said something totally unexpected/unbeliev-able, you might have to do some swift damage repair without the time to take instructions from me. As a former professional sol-dier, I would not expect you to tell me where to put my machine guns on the battlefield. You cannot accept me telling you what tactics to employ in the heat of the courtroom battle. Explain the ins and outs of Legal Aid and why and how you have duty to the Board. If you get it wrong, the Board will complain about you (it has) to the dreaded Complaints Commissioner. Tell me if there are any grounds for Appeal but explain how that works. Do not leave me in the lurch even if I am in a state of shock after sentence, but take care not to raise my hopes unrealistically. What different responsibilities you and the solicitor have. You are the consultant; the solicitor, the GP. If you can (I know it is difficult), explain why the judge and jury reached the extraordinary decision they did.

Then:

Do not ignore me when in conference with instructing so-licitors. Ask me my views even if they are ludicrous – "with the greatest respect" is a marvellous pre-amble to a sentence com-pletely demolishing my contribution. Show what a complete grasp you have of what, to me, is Byzantine in its complexity. But do not do it so arrogantly that I just think you are too clever by half. I know you are, otherwise you could not possibly have become a barrister. The *really* clever thing is not to show it. Look after me, lots of eye contact, shake hands (you are now allowed to, even with other barristers) and mentally pat me on the head or put an arm round my shoulder. I am terrified, I need it. If you are reaching a satisfactory, very sensible and advantageous agreement with your opponent, tell me about it. I am very suspicious of little deals being done behind my back. Do not talk in jargon to me. A Calderbank offer is something I might pick up on a good day at Tescos and a McKenzie Friend is someone who supports Scottish devolution as far as I know. I cannot spell affidavit nor have the first idea what it is. Get your clerks to answer letters/calls on your behalf. I do not know the convention that barristers do not correspond directly (for very good reasons) with lay clients. I just think it is bad manners. If you think I am going to be 'difficult' make sure someone takes good notes at the time of the conferences. I know the Insurers might suck their teeth but, if you are late or flustered or whatever, do say sorry. If you do not, much worse could happen. I never cease to be amazed by the public thoroughfare shambles outside courtrooms and the lack of private 'facilities'. Keep your voice down; people hear things they should not.

So much for the first year. I'd come through relatively unscathed but there were some personal Pooh Traps lying in wait, particularly with murderous intentions.

4

Murder

HAVING LED A RELATIVELY sheltered life, apart from some fairly vigorous soldiering, murder had played little part – until now. Perhaps a flavour therefore, at this stage, covering the rougher entries in my notebook, would be appropriate.

What one might call a long distance complaint came from a killer on death row in Trinidad. It was well outside the jurisdiction of the Bar and I told him so. 'Barrels' and 'scraping' were words which came to mind but full marks for tracking me down from his, I imagine, notorious prison. Trinidad and Tobago had more than 30 people on death row. The last executions there took place in 1999, when 10 men were hanged. It is one of only two Caribbean countries (the other being Barbados) that retains a mandatory death penalty for murder. Then there was the genuine article gunman. He was appealing on the grounds that he was arrested merely holding the sawn-off shot gun for his friend, as a favour, in the pub car park. The fact that the gun had recently been fired and two empty cartridge cases were found under a car didn't help. It was certainly an uphill struggle for his defending barrister. Admiration is hardly the word but I do have a mildly soft spot for the unreconstructed villain. I was able, confidently; to dismiss his complaint without help from the PCC as it was pretty clear this was a try-on with little hope of success. Writing of sawn-off shotguns reminds me of a fellow officer cadet at Sandhurst who was commissioned into the Life Guards. Short of cash, he fell in with some low-lifes and robbed a bank. He used one of his pair of Purdey shotguns, with the barrel sawn off. He was apprehended by the police without much difficulty. The judge was so appalled at the damage done to an extremely valuable shotgun, probably, outweighing the value of the loot, that he failed to send the miscreant to prison. The more scurrilous newspapers allege it was because they were both wearing Old Etonian ties.

Occasionally I had a complaint from someone really dissatisfied with the result of a murder trial where the defendant received something less than a life sentence. The complaint was usually from a member of the victim's family who were thirsting, understandably, for blood and revenge. The blame fell firmly on the perceived inadequacy of the prosecutor representing the Crown Prosecution Service (CPS). There was a feeling that crept up on me that barristers rather looked down on those employed by the CPS. This was totally unjustified when these people did a hard and unrewarding job for rather less than their more glamorous colleagues. The length of a sentence is often difficult for a layman to understand and it is influenced by so many factors. I was in no position to assess whether the prosecutor had made a nonsense nor, indeed, did I have the ability to explain the whys and wherefores to a complainant. I most certainly needed advice from a criminal specialist member on the PCC. The criminal barristers liked to call themselves 'criminal hacks'. It was a sort of depreciative expression to differentiate themselves from the vastly earning colleagues in, say, Chancery (whatever that is; no one ever complained about a Chancery barrister, so I don't know). I would take their advice and then try to pacify the complainant if the prosecutor had done his best. It seldom worked as the sense of grievance was almost insoluble; nothing less than hanging was what they were after. I could see their point and, while I accept capital punishment is no longer appropriate for all the reasons we know, one does sometimes feel the world would be better off without some of the most diabolical murderers.

In dealing with these cases, I really had to immerse myself in the detail of the case and try to put myself in the position of the complainant on one hand and the barrister on the other. Of course, I had no legal training, so was applying, basically, commonsense (I hoped) and a degree of experience of my previous life in taking difficult decisions. Often things would not be clear initially and I'd have to go back to the complainant to seek clarification; in legal slang 'Further & Better'. Most of the time I was not dealing with the Brain of Britain and this could be difficult but I did have the benefit of being able to put things, hopefully, clearly without obscure legal jargon. When I obtained the barrister's comments and their instructing solicitors' response, I could start, with luck, to balance the whole thing up. Often I would have a beautifully drafted Opinion from an expert PCC member. It was almost too clever for the recipient, so I'd split the infinitives and pretend it was mine.

There was a complaint against the prosecutor because the killer only got 15 months' sentence. Naturally, the complainant didn't explain all the ramifications of the case and what mitigation there might have been. When I asked the barrister prosecuting, he made it clear that it is the judge who imposes the sentence, not him. For safety, I went to a PCC member who endorsed what the accused barrister had maintained. There was a lot more to it than on first look but I agreed with the complainant that 15 months seemed inadequate, so I hope I managed to explain why.

A last gasp came from a multiple killer, with a number of life sentences, who had, over four years complained against any barrister he could think of; defending or prosecuting. He had attempted the Appeal system with no joy. He gave me an enormous amount of detail, including some pretty horrific accounts of the murders, all, of course, fully justified in his mind. He'd amassed all the correspondence with his solicitors, grounds of appeal drafted by barristers and the judges' reasons for rejection. With nothing to do in prison, the worm had eaten into his brain and convinced him that something must have gone wrong. After some consider-

MURDER

able time spent in going through the documentation, I could firmly see that there was nothing in the complaint and dismissed it but it did take a lot of time reading a copious amount of paperwork.

Another, whose son had been murdered, was incandescent that the alleged killer went free. I did have sympathy purely on what he'd told me. On the face of it something had gone very wrong. Consequently, I investigated it and, it was clear, from what the barrister said, there was doubt sown into the jury's mind by a very astute defence. A not guilty verdict was inevitable. You don't actually have to be a lawyer to see how some of this happens. Anyone can attend a trial from the public gallery. It is real, free, theatre although can be unbelievably boring when m' learned friends are immersed in the financial depths of a case. Murder is, however, better than the movies. In one such, an indignant individual, sitting, happily, in the public gallery was identified, by name, by the prosecuting barrister in the court. Highly indignant, he came to me. I asked why he felt aggrieved? It transpired he was a 'colleague' of the accused but in no way, naturally, involved in the crime for which his chum was in the dock. Was it actually illegal to point someone out in court or, indeed, in the public gallery? Technically, according to the PCC, it wasn't. However, it was a flamboyant act by a showing off barrister, which the more conservative members would marginally disapprove. I couldn't, of course, say that to the complainant – although tempted – but lean on the actual law i.e. the barrister wasn't wrong to do so, and dismissed it. I received a reply telling me exactly what the complainant thought of me. Luckily, he and his colleagues don't know where I live.

A tariff is set which means the offender is given a specific number of years they have to serve in prison before they can be considered for parole/release. Not unnaturally, this can become the basis of a complaint and argument with me as to the length of the tariff. I had to become a bit of an expert; not the steepest of my learning curves but quite technical and I had to be sure I was absolutely fireproof. Very often I would need help from a criminal barrister on the PCC.

From time to time, the letter starts, 'I have had certain legal advice…' As the postal address is HMP Wormwood Scrubs, the advice is probably from the chap in the next door cell. Michael is the most common first name among inmates in men's prisons, with 1,777 of England and Wales's 82,000 male prisoners sharing the name, so I'm in good company.[11]

After a bit, I developed a good sense, from the language, whether the advice came from a qualified lawyer or from the bloke in the porridge queue. Having said that, there some very experienced criminals in jail who, in the real world, had they gone straight, would have made good lawyers themselves. So I always took the 'advice' seriously, just in case.

A lady married a child killer in jail then had cold feet on his release. (There is some psychological explanation why women fall for criminals in jail but, I'm glad to say, well outside my remit). The killer didn't see it that way and wanted to resume his relationship. This turned out to become a case of extremely unpleasant stalking and victimisation of the woman. She then obtained an injunction against him to stop it and blamed the barrister when the killer took no notice and continued to plague her. It wasn't the fault of her barrister who had arranged the injunction but he could have given her proper advice on what her options were when her nemesis flaunted it. However, from what she told me, he and his solicitor were no longer instructed so I could only dismiss the complaint against the specific barrister. It was certainly not my job to advise anyone but I could hint, as I did here, that she should seek further legal help with fresh solicitors. I did have a sneaking sympathy; something about the course of true love never did run smooth….

A defendant can be allowed to appeal, depending on the judge who will agree or not, and has to explain his decision. It is not always allowed because there are rules which govern it and the chances of success have to be weighed. I didn't have to be aware of those rules, merely if the complainant was appealing or not. The first shot is to a Single Judge and, if that doesn't work,

11. *The Times* 7 May 2022.

up the scale to the Full Court of three judges. While appeals are on-going, I have to adjourn investigation to avoid any prejudice. The complainant always hopes that I'll support his complaint first thus manipulating the appeal system. When a complainant has exhausted the appeal system, I'm a sort of further resort. One could say that it is flattering to be thought of superior to the Full Court but, I'm afraid, that is not true; I'm much more akin to the Last Chance Saloon. When I am investigating a case such as this, I invariably ask to see the Judgement of the Appeal Court. It is highly unlikely that I am going to overturn such. A classic was a case of attempted murder for which the defendant got 14 years. He had been right through the whole system, including the Full Court, with which I wasn't going to disagree.

A murderer did send me the Judgement of the Full Court but it was 18 months out of date, so dismissed on those grounds. Our system had to have deadlines otherwise we'd be asked to look at ancient woes. It worked on the whole and people understood it but there was always someone who thought it worth a try even though we'd sent them the entire bumph about what our rules were.

Another gunman and arsonist, undergoing 9 life sentences for murder, thought his counsel was late in drafting his appeal. He wasn't, the miscreant simply didn't get permission to appeal. He'd conveniently overlooked this important detail when contacting me. It was very clear immediately I investigated the barrister and his instructing solicitor. What a surprise. When the appeal is refused, I'm certainly not going to go against the clearly expressed decision by a judge. I was more tolerant of an inmate of Broadmoor, who had great difficulty in expressing himself. It wasn't going anywhere but his solicitors were very helpful in outlining the problem and, most importantly, fully supporting their barrister.

This always made my life that much easier with seldom any need to approach a PCC member. It is the duty of barrister to explain to their clients the pure unvarnished truth. It is incompetent to pussyfoot around and wrap things up in so much cotton wool that clients get completely the wrong idea. When a barrister is, rightly, firm this can be construed as 'bullying'. For instance, there was the case of the prosecutor 'bullying' a father of a murdered son to accept the accused being charged with manslaughter rather than murder. Usually, the barrister knows what he is doing and can balance the chances of a prosecution sticking but it does nothing for the complainant's blood pressure. Here, the barrister is not, of course, representing the boy's family; the father is not his client and he has no 'duty of care' for him. He is the prosecutor but a good barrister will explain to those closely interested, what is happening, within the rules. Nevertheless, in a case such as this, I definitely need advice from the PCC. Did the barrister listen to the father? How much should he reveal to the father how he was going to prosecute the alleged murderer? In the end, it was clear that the barrister had behaved properly and I could dismiss it but, deep down, I had sympathy for the father. How would I react if someone murdered my son?

In the murderous world in which we live, there are still surprises, like the man who pushed another under a train. His defence was that it was an accident in a crowded underground during rush hour. He simply could not see why his barrister didn't get him off. The barrister had a tough row to hoe when it transpired that the someone the accused had pushed, was having an affair with his wife. Try as he might, the defence was in difficulties to persuade the jury that this had happened by chance. I believed the jury as well and dismissed it. I keep well clear of the platform edge when travelling on the Central Line to my office in Chancery Lane – just in case.

Another shot a raider in his house with a Glock pistol. He got 8 years. Something was clearly wrong even if, on the face of it, a man is allowed to defend his castle. To own a Glock, however, is unusual to say the least. These are particularly good close protection weapons, favoured now by the army and armed response police squads. Older military readers will be familiar with the Browning 9mm, which it replaced. Not something you pick up at Tescos. Personally, I prefer the Heckler & Koch MP 5, which has real stopping power. (I don't own one, says he quickly). It was

MURDER

much favoured by the close protection boys in Northern Ireland but difficult to conceal. In this case I certainly sought advice because, I suspect like most people, I believe you are perfectly within your rights to protect your home and loved ones. However, there is a line and this individual had well overstepped it. It's one thing to seize the nearest poker to defend yourself, it's quite another to give the intruder a magazine's worth of rounds from a Glock. The Criminal Law (Protection of Property) Bill introduced in the House of Commons in 2005 made a new defence available to a person who had used force in the prevention of crime, or in self-defence, or defence of another or of property, against an intruder in a building. It would provide an absolute defence unless the force used was grossly disproportionate.

During the last 20 years, cases in which intruders and people trying to tackle them have been injured or killed had fuelled debate about whether the existing law struck the right balance between the intruder and the householder. The law allows a person to use reasonable force in self-defence, or the prevention of crime, but it had been suggested that it was not clear to people what this meant. There had also been suggestions that the law did not give enough protection to a person who found intruders in his home. The case of Tony Martin (not the complainant I'm talking about), who shot an escaping burglar in the back and was convicted of manslaughter, was an extreme case which attracted a great deal of publicity, but there had been other cases in which decisions to charge or prosecute householders had been criticised. A press campaign to change the law was launched after a man was killed at his home by a burglar he had disturbed. The Bill would not affect cases like Tony Martin's, where the degree of force used had been grossly disproportionate. Martin was a farmer in Norfolk, who shot a burglar dead in his home in 1999. There was much sympathy for him. However, there was doubt cast on his evidence and it was revealed that he did not have a valid firearms certificate. He was initially convicted of murder, later reduced to manslaughter on grounds of diminished responsibility and served three years in prison, having been denied parole. The Government's view was

45

that the existing law was sound, and that the key was to ensure that householders understood it. As part of efforts to clarify the law and improve public understanding, the Crown Prosecution Service published advice to householders on the use of force against intruders. How would you behave on finding a burglar, or worse, in your house?

A cuckolded husband tried to run over his rival with his car. It was a triangular love story much used by authors of romantic novels. To pretend it was traffic accident didn't fool the jury for long. His barrister did his best and was well supported by his instructing solicitors, I could safely dismiss.

My day is made by stories straight out of the *Godfather*. Threats to witnesses, with blood-curdling consequences, are stuff of Don Corleone territory. My favourite was a notorious killing in Essex, when three very bad gangsters were brutally murdered in a Range Rover on a quiet country lane. All three of them were killed at close range with a shotgun, lying blood-covered and slumped in the vehicle until they were discovered by two local farmers the next morning. It was more than two years after the murders when the killers were convicted. Labelled as "execution-ers" by the judge, the two men were found guilty of blasting the three drug dealers to death in their Range Rover following a trial at the Old Bailey. They each received three life sentences with a minimum of 15 years. Secretly, I had to admit to some admiration for the courage of the killers, creeping up to the Rover and elim-inating all three at once, knowing full well what they were in for if discovered. The police tracked the mastermind through mobile phone transmissions. Now commonplace, at the time, criminals hadn't fluffed how vulnerable they were to this technology. Today they merely throw away a 'burner'. Mr Big, serving serious lengths in HMP Belmarsh, produced an immaculate binder, beautifully typewritten, with annexes and 'flags', which would have inspired envy from students at the Army Staff College. He complained against his defending Silk and Junior *and* the Prosecution Silk and his Junior. Imagine the power he must have exerted in prison to have this sort of thing done for him. I couldn't help imagining him as an immaculate Noel Coward being cheered by the inmates in prison in *The Italian Job*. It was far too elegant a complaint for me not to share it with a criminal Silk on the PCC. I also had to be extremely careful with the wording of my dismissal. Any chink would be exploited by this mega star of the prison firmament.

However, there were other threads in my tapestry.

5

Threads from the Tapestry

PEOPLE WHO COMPLAIN about barristers come in many hues - as many and varied as the threads of the Bayeux tapestry. They range from judges (surprisingly), to demanding debt-collectors, to hobbyists. (One of the latter informed me his primary hobby was collecting gold coins; his second, complaining about the legal profession. I told him to stick to the first - probably more rewarding). However, in the light of first year's experience, I was asked whether I detected a common theme running through complaints that would cause disquiet to the Bar Council or, indeed, major concern to the barristers themselves? Despite my antennae being alert to this, I failed to find a seam of complaints of worrying similarities. But, and there is always a but.

While complaints vary widely, the majority tended to come from three main sources. The Prisoner: "If my barrister had called the six witnesses I wanted and asked the questions I told him to, my sentence would have been halved". In a Divorce: "If my barrister had been half competent, I, not the wife, would have got the car." The Neighbour: "If my barrister had done his homework, he would have realised my garden was six inches longer in 1832." Do not forget though, mine is a very one-sided job. Presumably, there are many happy people, from the other side of the coin, running around extremely chuffed with their counsel - I just do not see them. No one tells me how good their barrister was.

Having said all that, there were things that regularly came up. It was not that the barrister had gone wrong but there were areas in which the client's nerve seemed to have been touched more than others. There were three that, with a layman's diffidence in telling a professional how to do his job, I offered barristers for, perhaps, further consideration. I stressed these were not the "seams" I mentioned earlier because, while they might have been the stuff of complaints, they seldom produced evidence of misconduct or inadequacy sufficient to attract the attention of the Professional Conduct and Complaints Committee; that "shiver looking for a spine to run up."[12]

The first was the wrong Opinion/Advice. The rules were clear on how counsel should write his Opinion. The trouble was, understandably, the client did not like bad news. The barrister must explain how he arrived at his conclusion and his duty to the Legal Aid Board if the case was being publicly funded.

Complainants often thought the barrister had written an adverse Opinion, deliberately to deprive them of "their" Legal Aid Certificate. If it helps, counsel should make it clear that the Board has absolutely no hesitation in complaining to the Bar Council if it thinks the barrister has taken a chance. Be cruel to be kind early on, but explain. The Legal Aid Board was responsible for the administration of Legal Aid. It was replaced in 2000 by the Legal Services Commission. Legal aid can help meet the costs of legal advice, family mediation and representation in a court or tribunal. It needs to be to be shown that the case is eligible for legal aid, the

12. Allegedly said by Harold Wilson of Edward Heath.

problem is serious and the individual cannot afford to pay for legal costs. Legal aid could cover a family at risk of abuse or serious harm, for example domestic violence or forced marriage, or a risk of homelessness. It could cover an accusation of a crime, facing prison or detention. It might apply to cases of discrimination or Human Rights. To deal with this a barrister must have a Legal Aid Certificate allowing him/her to do so.

At stages throughout their career, many barristers regard Pro Bono Legal Work as an integral part of being a member of the legal profession in providing access to justice and meeting unmet legal needs. It is one of the many different kinds of charitable works that barristers undertake. It covers legal advice or representation provided to individuals and community groups who cannot afford to pay for it and where public funding is not available. It is only an adjunct to, and not a substitute for, a proper system of publicly funded legal services. Believe it or not, I've actually had complaints against a barrister even when operating Pro Bono. It is not an uncomplicated world and I had a pompous Member of Parliament ordering me to explain it. I passed him swiftly to the Chairman of the PCC who would do rather better than me.

Secondly, the pressurised Guilty Plea. "If my barrister had not bullied me into pleading guilty, I would not be here now." I imagine briefing a client on the advantages and disadvantages of a plea must be extraordinarily difficult and requires the sensitive touch of a Florence Nightingale with the harsh reality of the firing squad. As we know, the final decision is the client's but, hindsight not always being beneficial, it is the wise barrister who has his client's decision witnessed by his instructing solicitor and his Back Sheet (his formal instructions from the solicitor) signed to that effect. An important point is that even if the client confesses *confidentially* to his barrister that he 'did it', the barrister cannot put in a 'not guilty' plea. The world of mitigation then opens up.

Thirdly, and allied to the one above, the unagreed Consent Order. Being human we hear what we want to hear and read what we want to read. After a long, difficult and complicated day in Court, all we want to do is to go home, and forget it all. We think, probably because we missed a crucial point, that we got the house/ car/premium bonds. Later, when we see the typed Order, it leaves out the bit we think important. I recall one such complaint, when it was a matter of one hour's difference in pick up time on a Saturday morning in a child contact case. No big deal, you will say, but it certainly was to the complainant, and matrimonial practitioners will know what one hour means in these super-heated negotiations. Does 'one hour on a Saturday morning' mean 0900-1000 or, say, 1100-1200? It could make all the difference to someone's travel arrangements for example. So, ensure the client knows - to the letter - what he is consenting to and do not allow him/her to rush off before it is absolutely crystal clear.

Finally, barristers complained about, rightly, sometimes feel a bit beleaguered. They have done their best and then feel that a complaint against them is unwarranted and unfair. It is highly personal and, usually, against them, not their Chambers, the Judges, the Bar Council or the Law. It can be very isolating and sometimes difficult to share with colleagues or friends and family. I know, because when I have dismissed a complaint the laser beam is occasionally swivelled onto me. However, I have the benefit of the very close support of the Secretariat and know that, when I get into real trouble, which I have done, I have the full support of the Bar Council. Recently, a dissatisfied complainant wrote, calling me a "useless geriatric". As I had just passed my 58th birthday and my aching muscles were gradually recovering from a week's skiing with my 28 year-old son, who takes no prisoners on the slopes, this remark touched a tiny nerve. Anyway - how did he know I was that old?

Perhaps a few items from my notebook will illustrate the wide variety of the life of this 'useless geriatric'.

Sadly, there is no such thing as a 'vexatious complainant'. If there was, a number of my correspondents would qualify. There is a 'vexatious *litigant*' which, while it has parallels, is not quite the same thing. Vexatious litigants are individuals who persistently take legal action against others in cases without any merit. They are then forbidden from starting civil cases in courts without permission. To stop a vexatious individual litigant issuing repeated applications, an Extended Civil Restraint Order can be brought against them. What you don't want is a Vexatious Litigant acting as a McKenzie Friend. It sometimes happens because they are the same sort of people.

Unusually, I had a difficult, obstinate and lazy judge who refused to comment on a complaint when I sought his views.[13] He merely told me to get tape recordings of the hearing. This is expensive and not my responsibility. It is that of the complainant. However, the judge could have helped. Luckily, I don't have to deal with this kind of petulant arrogance very often. Not a candidate for the Supreme Court methinks. My money was much more on the judge who replied to my question about what a complainant alleged, 'So contrary to what I conclude was intrinsically probable as to be incapable of belief.' I developed a technique for dealing with elderly, slightly dotty senior citizens, who, on the whole, were just getting cross about something. They would receive my 'old soldier' letter. This was, basically, I'm one of you (partially true, I was nearing my Bus Pass qualification) and I do understand the iniquities of the modern world having roughed it in bad climates in different parts of the globe. This tended to develop into a bit of a pen-pal relationship which really wasn't what the Bar paid me for.

We had a complaint from someone suffering from MS. Not unnaturally, I had great sympathy in these, very few, kinds of cases. We had a few good sorts around the country who were rather like Soldiers, Sailors, Airmen and Families Association (SSAFA) visitors when I was in the Army, to call on the individual. They weren't employed by the Bar but we covered their expenses. They were invaluable in a crisis. Sadly, in this case, the complainant refused the visit which made life very difficult for everyone. There was a deaf dyslexic complainant. It took an hour to complete the complaint form over the telephone. It was a very difficult and sad

---

13. I was firmly in the camp of FE Smith, later the Earl of Birkenhead, when he was called by the judge 'extremely offensive'. 'As a matter of fact, we both are, the only difference between us is that I am trying to be, and you can't help it'.

case, in which solicitors were involved trying to help. We did our best, leading to the withdrawal of the complaint. Another one was from a blind, disabled Chinese takeaway shop owner. He was interviewed by one of our staff, trying to help, and it worked. The visitor did not reveal whether he'd got a buckshee takeaway on the strength of it.

We were, flatteringly, asked for advice from the Department of Army Legal Services (DALS) concerning a barrister officer. When I was serving, we always regarded the DALS with a certain amount of suspicion. Were they failed barristers or were they barristers who fancied a life roughing it outside Chancery Lane? The first time I tried to pass the Staff College entry exam (failed) you had to sit a Military Law paper. As this was well outside my experience, I attended a short Military Law course. I had a very well built, jovial Lieutenant Colonel instructor. Sadly, the only thing I remember being taught was the Anglo Saxon word for punching a hole in armour. The other, rather more polite, four-letter word I used was PLOM; shorthand for Progression of Litigation by Other Means. This referred to the many complainants who had exhausted every legal means available to them and I was the final hope. However, when a complainant failed to respond to three of my letters, so I dismissed, it had an electrifying effect with a letter by return registered post.

Having had my fingers burnt with Public Relations, which I explained earlier with the lion cubs in Kenya, I supped with journalists with a long spoon. Nevertheless, part of my job was to demonstrate to the media the workings of the complaints system. It was not something that I enjoyed but it was the proper thing to do; for example the annual Press Conference, which I covered earlier. The Bar Council had a public relations consultancy company which would provide advice particularly when the barristers found themselves uncomfortably exposed to the media. I happily used the firm when the PR light fell on me. I featured on the radio programme *You & Yours*. It was a respected programme in the world of lifting stones to expose iniquity and genuinely helping people at their wits' end. It was not one, though, I was very familiar with as it went out in the mornings when I was slaving at my desk. I tried my best but it didn't really work. What I wanted to do was explain how we did our work and how complaints were fairly handled. However, it didn't happen like that. After a brief introduction, I was phoned on line by aggrieved complainants and, because of the confidentiality rules, had to be rather opaque in my responses. I couldn't go into the detail of a case which, of course, was what the caller wanted. They don't like that on *You and Yours*. It became a bit heated and I didn't come out of it too well. I was not asked again.

One of the conventions amongst barristers is that they never shake hands with each other. The custom, presumably, dates back to sword-bearing times, when a handshake was considered a way to demonstrate to a person that you were not armed. Since barristers were gentleman, they trusted each other implicitly, and therefore there was no need to shake hands to prove they were not armed. Fine, as long as you know the person you meet is a barrister. I recall, on being introduced to an elderly barrister at a soirée in Lincoln's Inn, holding out my hand, which he wouldn't shake until his companion told him I wasn't a barrister.

The office of 'Lord Chancellor' came to an end and is now the 'Department of Constitutional Affairs,' known to its friends as 'DECAFF.' It's rather sad as I had an illustrious forbear, John Scott, the 1st Earl of Eldon, who was Lord Chancellor in the early 19th century. His brother, William, also a lawyer, both of Middle Temple, became Lord Stowell. His house, Stowell Park in Gloucestershire, was sold to the Vestey family in 1926. Eldon made an enormous sum of money which, by the time it filtered down through the generations to my level had dwindled to nothing.

I once attended an excellent cocktail party hosted by a barrister with many of his barrister friends. I was, of course, a bit of an outsider and when guests found out what I did, I detected a slight *cordon sanitaire* around me. Anyway, trying to keep my end up, I boasted to one, of my ancestral heritage and how, really, I was one of them. 'Ah, good,' he said, 'the Y chromosome'. I had to look it up.

THREADS FROM TAPESTRY

The Residential Property Tribunal Service sought advice on our procedure and sanctions. I wasn't quite sure whether this corralled estate agents (very unlikely) or something else. It was always interesting to be asked by other regulatory organisations for advice as it showed how their systems worked, or, usually, didn't. Sadly, members of the Iraqi Bar Delegation, who were after guidance, never made it as their visit to us was cancelled due to Baghdad airport being closed. It was under mortar fire from insurgents. Much later I briefed some senior Army officers, who were trying to set up some sort of complaints system in the Army. Their initial stab at it was not going to work simply because it had no teeth. In the first instance the complaint was referred back to the Commanding Officer who was, probably, the person complained of. The Probation Service always seemed to come in for a hard time as the public were only ever aware of the nonsense it occasionally made; not all the good work which consistently went on. However, I was not impressed with a probation officer who complained about a barrister complaining about him. I forget who was worse.

Occasionally, people became exasperated with something that has gone wrong and, tearing their hair out, find me. Here was a gardener who didn't get paid by a barrister for work done on his garden, so tried to use our system to get at him. I had some sympathy. It was clearly a civil matter and nothing to do with me but the pompous barrister wrote a quasi legal letter, signing himself Barrister-at-Law. That did it. The barrister was fined £75 by an Adjudication Panel.

There was a ridiculous complaint by man who infringed security at a US base in England after the 9/11 Twin Towers attack. He objected to a certain amount of rough handling and complained his barrister hadn't properly represented him and wanted to sue the American Government for £20,000. Given understandable American sensitivities, he was probably lucky to emerge in one piece. I had absolutely no sympathy and it probably showed in my dismissal letter. Off he went, of course, to the LSO, who supported me with an even briefer response.

Rather like the man who, in a letter to me, used the word 'pellucid' when he meant 'very clear'. I think people, because they were dealing with barristers, or little off-shoots like me, tried to use flowery language to be on a par, so to speak, with the address-ee. My reaction was to write back in seriously basic language. Sometimes it worked in that there was some relief from the complainant that he didn't have to match the (assumed) brain power of the barrister. A man with possibly the same amount of brain cells, failed to turn up as prosecution witness then complained that the barrister did not Judicially Review the magistrates' decision. Even with my non-barrister intelligence, I couldn't see what he was getting at and why, if he hadn't bothered to get off his own bottom, how he could possibly complain. (I didn't actually use those words in my dismissal).

Royal Mail, unsurprisingly, came in for some hardship. Luckily, I didn't have to handle complaints against them. But what about the chap who was convicted in January 1994? He completed our form in July 1999 but forgot to post it until 28 July 2003. He blamed Royal Mail. Another claimed he sent us a letter but when we didn't reply, waited three months to say so. Oh dear.

The International Criminal Tribunal for Rwanda was an international court in Arusha, Tanzania, established by the United Nations Security Council in order to judge those responsible for the Rwandan genocide and other serious violations of international law in Rwanda, or by Rwandan citizens in nearby states, between January and December 1994. The court eventually convicted 85 individuals at a cost of $1.3 billion. (See my book with the chapter on Romeo Dallaire).[14] I received a complaint against one of the British barristers involved. It was extremely complicated but, luckily, outside our jurisdiction. As an afternote, it is not difficult to understand some disquiet about sending asylum seekers to Rwanda to start a new life.

Luckily, I can read quite fast as I received a 98 page complaint against the police. It was nothing to do with us but I had to

14. *Scapegoats – Thirteen Victims of Military Injustice.* Elliott & Thompson. London 2013.

read the lot just to make sure. I became very used to all kinds of written communication; green ink on lavender paper, torn sheets from notebooks, official prison writing paper, worn out typewriter ribbon, biro/big fat felt tips, red ink capitals, the odd upside down pages just to ensure I was awake and scruffy barely legible handwriting. Once I got a letter written on Bronco, the old fashioned loo paper. I thought it had long gone but maybe there was someone secreting a small cache in case it became a valuable number on Antiques Road Show. Or, alternatively, was it the complainant making a clever lavatorial point? It all had to be read just in case there was a nugget I needed to extract. I also received a fax (those were the days) dated Christmas Day. What a sad life the writer must be having. As the Bar Council offices hibernated between Christmas Eve and the day after New Year's Day, I didn't read it until 2 January which infuriated the complainant even more.

Very occasionally, I suffered from what the barristers call 'professional embarrassment'. This meant that I had some sort of connection, however peripheral, to the case. One such was a complaint involving a land dispute in Morden College, Blackheath.[15] The Chairman of the Trustees was a good friend of mine and, although nothing to do with him, I had to withdraw. What happened then was that it went directly to the PCC without my involvement. There was a complaint against former member of my Regiment, now a barrister. I did not serve with him so was not 'professionally embarrassed'. He was cleared of any misdeed.

I was sent a naughty *Private Eye* cartoon of a judge. This was accompanied by the complainant's (unprintable) comments on what he thought of the judge in question and the judiciary in general. I should have framed and kept it on my office wall. Incidentally, until I retired from the Bar Council in 2006, there was no procedure for complaining about a judge. This was set up after I left. The cartoon was followed by a supercilious letter from an MP about the Pro Bono Unit. I don't think he knew what Pro Bono

15. Morden College is a Charity dedicated to supporting older people. Founded in1695 by the pioneering merchant, Sir John Morden, the Charity has been at theforefront of enriching older people's lives.

meant – dog food? I should have framed that as well. Then Mr D, an old sparring partner, writes that he'll return all our letters unopened and not to waste his time further. Fine by me.

All happy families are alike, but every unhappy family is unhappy in its own way.[16]

I fear this is one where a father complains against his son who is a QC. How sad and bitter life has become for these two. I try to handle it as sensitively as I can without going through the formal process of the PCC. It did succeed but only after I felt as though I'd been through the wringer myself. However my day is brightened by Mr F. He sent me a Christmas card from sunny southern Spain. He was a Grenadier Guardsman complainant who, surprisingly, liked me. He had complained before and I had amicably solved it. I cannot remember what it was about but I don't think it really mattered. What was much more important to us both was that I'd probably let him know I was also a Guardsman. We soldier-boys must stick together.

A few complainants live in a world of their own. There was the dreaded Mr S. He'd made seven previous complaints under different names. I think this was his third or fourth pseudonym. We were becoming experts at fathoming out his choice of name based on his life experiences and relations with his animals. The names derived from what he'd had for breakfast to some classic Fido-type pets. To say nothing of the chap who claimed the late Queen was his aunt. Presumably he thought the Royal Family connection would assist his complaint. I could find no obvious lineage to the Monarch so, luckily, didn't have to seek her comments. This was closely followed by the man who thought abuse is only possible from the Ruling Classes to the Lower Orders. He didn't elaborate but guess where the barristers rate. Thankfully, he hadn't thought to ask what class I came from. Perhaps, like in India, there are castes. There must be a very low one for complaints handlers. Barristers are not immune to outbursts of temper. Michael, the security guard on front desk of our offices in the foyer downstairs, summoned me to help with a rude and aggressive bar

16. *Anna Karenina,* Leo Tolstoy, 1878

rister. (I can't remember why he was in such a state but it didn't matter). He was thoroughly obstreperous and I thought 'losing it' as they say on the Terraces. I obliged and rather enjoyed myself. I hasten to say that it didn't result in fisticuffs but the barrister saw the error of taking us both on. He retired, muttering under his breath, something about seeing us both in Court. He didn't.

I must finish this chapter with one of the major pieces of embroidery of this rich tapestry.

An A4 sized postcard arrived through the post, with a large heading in capitals, A POSTCARD OF SHAME. It was addressed to Sir Michael Scott, flattering but incorrect. It was copied to Lord Irvine, Lord Woolf and the Rt Hon David Blunkett MP. The reverse of the card was a diatribe against the Chief Executive of the Bar Council. Against me was a question of who paid my wages and where does the cash come from? Despite its wide distribution and an open communication, it cannot be published as it is 'property' of the Bar Council and therefore subject to confidentiality rules. The fact that it had been, probably, kicked around the floor of the Mount Pleasant Royal Mail sorting office, open to all readers, appeared to be irrelevant. So, sadly, I cannot disclose the contents from one of the more colourful complainants. Despite a lively exchange of letters, by May 2003, the bold Mr C and I had finally fallen out. He sent me Thirty Pieces of Silver,[17] but, because he'd designated me Rat of the Week (I wondered who the other contestants were for this prestigious award), they were only copper pennies. Evermore, I kept this little bag on the bookcase in my office for the interest of passers-by. Not unnaturally, there was a certain amount of cross-examination when coupled with the tin of Argentine corned beef.[18]

But Mr C wasn't the only little cross I had to bear.

---

17. Of course, the well-known blood money earned by Judas Iscariot for betraying Jesus Christ. In Hebrew culture, thirty pieces of silver was not a lot of money. In fact, it was the exact price paid to the master of a slave if and when his slave was gored by an ox. Not many people know that.
18. In the next chapter.

6
Ordinary Decent Crime

"ALLO MR SCOTT, I'M COMIN' to Lunnon to see me lady-friend and I'll drop in." Mr P's West Country charm penetrated the protective layers my inestimable PA wove around me. Mr P was one of my earlier 'clients', but not for him the boring bureaucracy of dates, diaries or appointments. He would arrive, unannounced, on one of his little forays to London. His actual complaint had long been forgotten by us both – something to do with the injustice of being made to pay VAT, I think.

Our original rapport really sprang from one of his visits when he told me he had been in a famous infantry regiment on D-Day. We spent a happy time, in a local pub, discussing the pros and cons of having your artillery observation post in a church spire and how close you could allow your supporting machine gun fire to get to your troops in the assault. Meanwhile back at the Bar Council….

ORDINARY DECENT CRIME

During my time in Northern Ireland, Ordinary Decent Crime (ODC) referred to crime other than terrorism. This chapter covers hardly anything decent – gangsterism, drugs, Grievous Bodily Harm, kidnapping etc but NO sex. That is for later. I also touch on my responsibility for recruiting lay representatives to the various panels; an essential part of the process of complaint handling.

Out of all the prisoners I dealt with, my preference was for the out and out, unreconstructed gangster. You tended to know where you stood. One wrote a veritable novel to me, except it was not entirely fiction. It was beautifully typed and produced, and he even had his own logo. This made a change from the chap who used to cut out the Bar logo from my letters and send it back to me, glued upside down on his reply. In dismissing his complaint, I told him he ought to take up writing. I think he was rather chuffed. He has probably even now got his own website; gangsters@belmarsh.com perhaps? But there were others, with drugs featuring highly.

A prisoner doing 9 years in HMP Parkhurst claimed he didn't know why he was in prison and blamed it on his barrister for not telling him. Surely even the doziest criminal must know what he's doing time for? Perhaps I should be flattered that he should think I might give him the answer? Maybe a convoluted way of escaping justice. If I can't tell him, then his conviction must be wrong and he gets out? He was actually doing time for shooting someone in another gang. Another had difficulties in writing letters from the Secure Unit HMP Frankland. Hardly surprising, I therefore gave him more time to respond. He was a multiple killer.

Next was a very unfocussed complaint by a father, originally in prison for drug offences, on behalf of a 21 year old son with the mental age of 14. There were many assertions of fraud, perversion of the course of justice etc. There was reliance on a police record of arrest and alleged pressurised confession. The complainant, with no evidence to support his case, asserted that Counsel bullied the boy to plead guilty with no appeal. He could have appealed but only against sentence. This was very difficult as, clearly, the father was trying his best for his son, who was unable to look after himself. We were only one cog in his campaign. It was really, I'm afraid, one for Social Services but it was worrying.

Another father, imprisoned for drug offences, complained that his son's handling by police in the cells was not raised in his defence. Complainant, a barrack room lawyer, knew it all from long service in prison himself. However, he might have been right so I had to investigate it. The barrister explained that the assertion, even if true, was not, realistically, going to assist the defence which was pretty rocky anyway.

With the unpleasant world of drugs, I start to become a bit of an expert. In my early days, I had to go to a member of the PCC for advice but as time went on I really got the feel of the drug world and how its denizens conducted their lives. On the whole, they weren't intellectual heavyweights and it didn't take long to see through the guff. A crack cocaine dealer having had his appeal turned down, turned to me. This often happened. When everything else had failed, I'm the last port of call. Same detail with a drug runner doing 11 years. A dealer undergoing 24 and 19 concurrent years' jail asserted that counsel for another defendant imputed dishonesty by *his* counsel. The tricky world of blaming the other defendant – the 'cut-throat defence'. However, it is quite something to accuse the other chap's barrister of crime. A drug baronet (a sort of low-level baron) is doing 9 years plus £200,000 compensation, which, understandably, he didn't like. The 200 grand was tucked away, he thought somewhere safe but no longer. It was probably a recovery by the State from the proceeds of crime. A drug trafficker, doing 22 years, argued against penalty of £1.2m or 10 years in lieu. He maintained Counsel should have got an accountant. So should I.

A drug runner relies on technical defence not used by his barrister. He might have been right, so I did have to go a PCC member. A rather more exotic cocaine importer from Jamaica has had his Full Court appeal refused, therefore I confidently dismiss. A little happier, a prisoner decided to plead guilty to an amended charge. He had already done time on remand and was therefore released in 3 weeks, so drops complaint. A drug smuggler warns me of Judicial Review as he didn't like my dismissal. Judicial review is a type of court proceeding in which a judge reviews the lawfulness of a decision or action made by a public body. In other words, judicial reviews are a challenge to the way in which a decision has been made, rather than the rights and wrongs of the conclusion reached. A clever criminal had heard of this and thought worth giving it a try. It was not an easy thing to do – thank goodness, otherwise they'd all be at it. A drug baronet helpfully sends us change of address from HMP Belmarsh to HMP Parkhurst, Isle of Wight. Is this downsizing or upgrading?

A crack cocaine merchant, doing 10 years with deportation on release, is impatient at lack of judgement of Full Court. I agree but the wheels turn… A drug baronet goes on trying even after Full Court and Criminal Cases Review Commission (CCRC). It is unusual to try this far. He must have time on his hands. A cocaine dealer was fined £85,000 and 10 years in the slammer. I'd seen the Full Court judgement, so dismiss. A prisoner doing 11 years, was 'Not allowed to plead guilty'. This was difficult to understand. If a client confesses to his defending barrister that he was guilty, the barrister is honour bound to advise him to plead guilty and do his best for him in mitigation etc. So wires had got crossed here somewhere. A drugs courier, doing 12 years, refused to send me a copy of the Full Court judgement. I reach the obvious conclusion and dismiss. A female drug bandit claims her appeal was drafted late. Indeed, there was criticism of her barrister by Court of Appeal. I therefore referred the case to the PCC. The barrister may have been reprimanded but that would not have 'corrected' the client's case; she'd have to go through the legal process to do that but it could have been a factor in her favour.

An interesting Turkish drug baron got 17 years for heroin possession. He had lots of 'previous' (convictions) for drug trafficking, so probably lucky to have got only 17 years. He faced deportation on release and, possibly, Turkish jurisdiction on arrival in his homeland, which was something he definitely did not want.

Finally, a foreign dealer gets 17 years. It is a very convoluted complaint written by someone else whose first language is not English either. Nevertheless, we did our best and wove through the unjoined up writing.

Away from the drug world there is a soupçon of smuggling and kidnapping.

A smuggler of cigarettes and drink could not understand the length of his sentence and confiscation order (of his booty) when others got less. To prove his case, he enclosed a number of newspaper cuttings. They proved nothing, just some of the rather more florid journalistic imagination. I contacted the complainant to seek clarification. I expected a carton of 200 cigarettes and a bottle of brandy at least. Sadly, this was met with evasion and complete failure to answer my questions. A kidnapper fails to respond to my last letter and two previous reminders. The letter is returned by the prison marked 'gone away'. Probably released rather than escaped. It may have been a warder with a sense of humour. A Russian blackmailer/kidnapper blames his defending barrister. This was the depths of murky 'political' gangland operations; real MacMafia stuff.[19] I was merely a small piece in the complex jigsaw puzzle. Another kidnapper got 8 years. He didn't like it as it wasn't really kidnapping as a such; merely 'taking someone away for a short period of time.' Shades of Robert Louis Stevenson.

Then there is lots of Grievous/Actual Bodily Harm.[20]

A vitriolic, and inarticulate, letter from a complainant whose son was doing 5 years for wounding with intent. He refused to accept my earlier dismissal, returning our pamphlet on how to approach the LSO, torn in half. I sent him another on the basis that the first one had been 'damaged in the post'. I doubt that he saw the joke. One of the documents I always find useful is

19. *McMafia* is a British crime drama television series. It is inspired by the book *McMafia: A Journey Through the Global Criminal Underworld* by Misha Glenny.
20. As an aside, when I was the General in Scotland, I lived in a large house on the outskirts of Edinburgh, called Gogar Bank House, not unnaturally abbreviated to GBH.

the official transcript of a case. A printout can be expensive and it is, luckily, not my job to buy one on behalf of a complainant. To support their case I sometimes advise them to show me the transcript. Occasionally they do so and it can be illuminating, as happened here with a habitual GBH prisoner trying his best to no avail. A complainant was very elastic with the truth over a GBH charge with a car. He neglected to tell me he got two months in jail for deliberately running someone over. Further clarification required. A complaint was made by a father over his son who was charged with GBH and intimidating witnesses. He claims prosecuting counsel used words not in the police statement but counsel maintains he was told that by the police. He was perfectly legitimate in using it but I did check with a PCC member. A very unpleasant assault with knife and baseball bat. The complainant is aggrieved at sentence, as well he might, but he doesn't tell me the details, so there is not much I can do. A vehicle clamper used GBH against a motorist and is now in HMP Wormwood Scrubs. I think he hit him with part of the clamping iron. However, he hasn't appealed. I suspect it was not allowed which is always a sign that the complainant was well and truly convicted. A gunman, who has now been released after a 3½ year sentence, tries to refer us to some tape. If relevant, it is his responsibility to produce the evidence to support his complaint. I had no idea what tape he was writing about. It faded into the distance. This chap got 4 years for 'glassing'. ('Glassing', for readers of a sheltered background, is smashing a glass or bottle and ramming the jagged edges into an opponent's face). He doesn't like the sentence and has tried his luck with the CCRC. I adjourn until I see what they say, rather like I do with appeals. It went nowhere.

I got into a little bit of trouble over a Pole who was doing time. One of our charming secretaries was Polish by birth though now a British citizen. I thought, with a view to being seen as fair, helpful and even-handed etc, I'd allow the prisoner to write to us in his own language and our secretary would translate it. This would save the Bar Council the expense of employing a professional interpreter, save time and have someone translate who knew the legal language niceties. Not so, I was told. It might be seen to be biased to use our own people and more transparent to use an outsider. I did what I was ordered but did gain some mild plaudits (translated by the secretary) from the Pole in prison.

The barrister, whom the complainant wanted, failed to turn up and he got another from same Chambers. Even in the best organised, this sometimes happens through sickness or the like. Clearly, very disappointing for a client who has got used to, and trusting, their counsel. The stand-in, however, would have got himself briefed up. An interesting complaint arrives, where the Full Court has quashed the conviction (for assault/affray/ threats to kill). This was unusual and, unsurprisingly, the complainant blamed CPS barrister although he might have been justified in having a go at his defending barrister. However, the grounds for quashing the conviction must have been persuasive. There is something in this, so off to the PCC. Our next charmer is some-one who has 20 previous for violence. While he got a conditional discharge for 2 years, 4 months before sentence, he didn't like the 18 months he'd already spent in the slammer. Bit of an expert but came to nothing. Another GBH practitioner set his girlfriend's hair on fire. He tells me he has obtained new advice – probably from cell next door - that counsel didn't defend him properly. I disagreed with his advice. He was lucky to have received the light sentence (in my view) that he did.

Then there was the sad woman who tried to incinerate Ken Dodd. She admitted setting fire to his home in Knotty Ash, Liverpool. The fire in October 2001 caused an estimated £11,000 damage to the ground floor of the property. She had shoved burning rags through the letter box. A more serious charge of arson with intent to endanger life was dropped by the prosecution. She admitted sending a dead rat earlier through the post.[21]

I'm afraid her defending barrister, against whom she complained, had a hard row to hoe and was not to blame for her conviction and sentence.

Occasionally, there is a deal. In this case a violent burglar got

21. *The Guardian* 5 March 2003.

off with just having to complete community service. He couldn't be bothered to turn up to do whatever he was meant to do and so is therefore now in prison and doesn't like it. Serves him right. A chancer hit a police officer with an iron bar and wonders why he got 7 years. Having read the evidence, I tell him and dismiss his grievance.

Lay Representatives.

One of the keys to our complaints handling system was the contribution of lay representatives. A quorum of them would attend the PCC meetings and be represented on the various disciplinary panels. They were a considerable asset. They were robust individuals, unawed by the professionals, who would ask commonsense, awkward and penetrating questions. They retained a veto over any dismissal by the PCC of a complaint so had considerable power. The barristers took them extremely seriously. It was my responsibility to recruit them. To fill 15 places, I recall sifting 377 applications. I reduced them down to 24 for interview with 11 reserves. I then interviewed candidates, flanked by a PCC barrister and a former lay representative. It worked extremely well, with one exception.

Mr A, I think, saw himself as a sort of barrister manqué. He argued points of law at PCC meetings, which were nothing to do with him, exasperated the barristers and embarrassed me for recruiting him. Later, I realised he was probably suffering from the Dunning-Kruger effect. He completely failed to grasp the burden of proof, which was not difficult, even for a layman. In frustration, I interviewed him in my office, supported by a lady barrister, who was charm itself to him. When he had left, she said to me, 'Mike, my father always warned me to beware of men wearing short socks.' Sitting opposite him, she'd been exposed to the small hairy leg above short white socks. He complained about the PCC, and, I think, me probably, to the LSO and when she sent him packing he tried to Judicially Review us. When that, inevitably, failed the Chairman of the Bar swore to seek costs next time. His three year contract was not renewed.

To finish on a lighter note, I had a complaint involving a

neighbourhood dispute over the right of way through a gate into a field. It was not actually a difficult legal matter to understand and the barrister acting for the complainant had, clearly, done a proper job. However, the complainant lost his case and, sure as eggs are eggs, came to me. After due investigation, with comments from the barrister and his instructing solicitor, I dismissed the case. I did not need expert advice and it certainly wasn't going anywhere near the PCC. There then started a barrage of vitriol, not the worst I'd suffered but a tiresome waste of time. At one point my persecutor wrote something along the lines of, 'What would have happened if we'd had useless cowards like you on the beaches at D-Day?' I thought this a little over the top, so replied, 'No, of course I wasn't on the beaches at D-Day. However, I was on Blue Beach, San Carlos Water, in May 1982, in the Falkland Islands war'.[22]

By return of post, I received a grovelling apology with 'present arrives under separate cover'. A few days later a parcel appeared, containing a tin of Argentine corned beef. I kept it on my bookcase alongside the Thirty Pieces of Silver. Clearly, I had established a *rapport* with this individual because, somehow, he discovered I was a fan of the Eddie Stobart trucking company. He may well have been a driver since, after the tin of meat, a Stobart tie, worn by their truckers, arrived. Just the job for Regimental reunions.

Thinking of tins, in 2002, 17,671 people required hospital treatment after trying to open tins, excluding those containing corned beef which alone accounted for 9,000 injuries.[23]

I imagine Personal Injury barristers must have been rubbing their hands with glee, as long as they hadn't tried to open one.

Next - to sex and marriage. Trigger warning for sensitive souls. As they say on TV news, 'Some scenes viewers may find upsetting'.

---

22. Technically it wasn't a 'war' but a 'conflict' as neither side had actually declared 'war' on the other. Pompous people sometimes liked to tell me that and my response was, 'From where I was standing, it was certainly a 'war'.
23. *The Spectator* 15 February 2003.

7

Sex raises its Ugly Head

TWO OF THE MOST DIFFICULT, and sometimes repellent, areas I had to deal with were complaints from sex offenders and those from aggrieved parties in matrimonial disputes.

Matrimonial difficulties – mainly about the financial settlement of a divorce and child custody – were handled by the inappropriately called Family Division. It was usually about the breakup of a family rather than Happy Families. In a world of the most bitter disputes and heartbreaking collapse of family life, it always astonished me how barristers could specialise in this arena. Being an absolute legal minefield, I often sought help from a PCC member. Having lost badly in court, the complainants then attempted to continue their campaign by coming to me. I was little help because, on the whole, the barristers knew what they were doing. What people forget is that a barrister can seldom right a wrong which has happened in someone's personal life. Barristers are not marriage guidance counsellors but negotiators and settlers of disputes.

Give me the hardened gangster any time.

Having, happily, come from a very stable family myself, it was an area pretty foreign to me and not part of the job I relished. However, I was very aware of the upsetting world my 'clients' inhabited, so tried to deal with things as sensitively as I could. Without becoming over involved, I very often had to go back to the complainant to understand the situation. Don't forget I was dealing with people who were going through enormous personal trauma and writing about it to a stranger (me) was not easy for them. It wasn't that easy for me either but I had to be absolutely clear on what the complaint was about. In the jargon of lawyers I was seeking 'F & B' – Further and Better. This did not, sadly, always have a happy ending.

Early on, I faced a matrimonial complaint over an Opinion and return of papers concerning residence and contact over a child. I had no response to my letters seeking clarification from the complainant – my F & B - and could only, therefore, dismiss the case with regret because I was no use to them. But they had to help me to help them. Another complainant wrote far too much detail about his child. It was stopped in its tracks before getting to me and the papers returned under the Children Act 1989. (Later, I learn, to my cost – a court appearance - in a separate case, the prohibition, under that Act, of anyone seeing papers concerning a child without the Judge's permission. I explain this in Chapter 10). This is, rightly, an extremely powerful law but the solution was relatively simple; the parent had to seek the Judge's permission to share the detail with anyone else i.e. us. Then there was a complaint of Byzantine complexity by solicitors accusing counsel of misquoting figures and overcharging in a divorce case. Luckily, I had nothing to do with charges made by barristers since it was purely a contract between their clerks and their instructing solicitors. All I could do was to refer the complainant back to the solicitors and, if not satisfied, which quite clearly they weren't, to contact the Law Society. Here, I didn't really have much sympathy; the solicitors were very professional lawyers who knew the ropes and were blatantly trying to 'use' me to further their own campaign.

A woman, in divorce proceedings, complained about her husband, who was a barrister. This was always tricky as I had to be sure that the complainant was not just using me as a weapon against her husband within the complaints system. I, therefore, had to look at each case extremely carefully to ensure this didn't happen and that the complaint was genuinely against the barrister for what he/she had done *as a barrister* not just as an opponent in a matrimonial case. In this case, I could do nothing as the barrister was disbarred. He had been convicted, by the Bar, of lying in Court. However, on appeal against his disbarment, he was re-instated with a 2½ year suspension. I therefore reactivated the complaint, although it was part of the divorce, her complaint, on the face of it, had been against him for what he did as a barrister. I had to determine whether this was a hangover from the lying in Court or a separate matter. In the end I concluded that the wife was still trying to fix him for lying for which he'd paid the penalty, so dismissed the complaint.

There was a disillusioned ex-husband, living in China, who had a go at three barristers. It was very difficult to unravel who was who and who was acting for whom. I sought help from the instructing solicitor who would only respond after authority from the barristers. He was not going to seek that authority but 'suggested' I did so. I hope I wasn't being unfair to conclude that the solicitor could not identify who was going to pay his fee for so doing. Weeks later, with to-ing and fro-ing from China, I finally managed to sort it out. This was a more practical scenario with, happily, very little emotion, merely a very cross chap in China.

There was a disappointed about-to-be ex-wife. However, on investigation, counsel was not well supported by his instructing solicitors. This is inevitably a bad sign. Ancillary relief is the polite name for what one party – usually the husband – has to give the other; alimony in the United States. It was unclear here as to what the husband had paid in mortgage and maintenance and how much was taken into account in Child Support. Although no expert, of course, in the intricacies, I immediately smelt a rat. The barrister was being deliberately opaque. It was far too difficult for me and steeped in matrimonial financial law so I sent it straight to a member of the PCC to unravel. From there, it went to a Disciplinary Tribunal. I was right.

Next, counsel disclosed confidential family matters to a solicitor with whom he was in a 'relationship'. This really was bad news. It certainly went to the PCC, with subsequent extreme discomfort for the barrister. In another parallel case, counsel revealed 'wife's' address at a Hearing. This should have remained confidential for obvious reasons. How could he do that? The barrister was properly at fault, therefore to the PCC. This was followed by a complainant who objected to being bullied by counsel for the Respondent into signing a false affidavit. What was 'false' about it? I had to investigate it though I suspected he was trying to progress the divorce but may have been a bit fly. I had, obviously, to read the affidavit, ask the complainant to identify the 'false' bits and question the barrister and his instructing solicitors what they had to say about it. My first suspicions turned out right in the end. After much 'F & B' the complainant ultimately capitulated.

A grandmother wanted the child to live with her rather than her 'useless daughter-in-law'. The judge refused her application – a real Solomon decision. Isn't there an old saying that individuals don't choose their in-laws? It was certainly the case here. Granny blamed counsel at length and he replied to me with one of the best responses I have seen. Of course, I showed what he'd written to Granny and, while I don't think she'd ever be satisfied with the outcome for her grandchild, I hoped I had, to a certain extent, showed her that in extraordinary difficult circumstances the barrister had behaved entirely properly. So I was able, in what were the most sensitive words I could muster, to dismiss her complaint. Now a grandfather myself I fully understood and sympathised with the grandmother.

There was a significant complaint against counsel on the

other side in a child contact hearing; rude, bullying and intimidatory. In the emotional atmosphere of the Families Court, people forget that it is the judge's responsibility to ensure this does not happen. It is really too late in the day to come to me with this sort of thing which should be dealt with on the spot. Was it a weak judge? In these few cases, the judge tended to be defensive and resented my enquiries. But I ploughed on and investigated the case. The barrister did not come out of it well and there was significant evidence to support the complaint. I remember the PCC, when the case was heard, to be very critical of the judge as well as the barrister. Many of the members were Recorders, or part-time judges themselves. So they knew the form.

A doctor had a child by a female doctor who was married to another doctor and wanted a 'closer' relationship with the mother of the child. I was not sure how this was going to work out but none of my business. What was my business was that he complained of intimidation against counsel for the still-married-to-the-mother doctor. The fragile world of happy families; I had to draw a little chart for myself to work it out. After much F & B, it was clear that the barrister had been 'robustly' acting for his client and while may not have had the honeyed tones of a TV sitcom lawyer (the late and much loved Donald Sinden, for example), he could not have been said to have been 'intimidatory'. However, just to be on the safe side, I passed it to one of the matrimonial experts on the PCC. She endorsed my view.

I chaired an Adjudication Panel. In this case counsel should have known child abduction law better and given different advice to his client. I had dealt with the complaint in the initial stages before it went to the PCC with the subsequent decision to refer it to the Adjudication Panel. Even with no technical knowledge of abduction law, there was something fishy about it. I was, of course, guided by the barrister member of the Panel. The barrister was ordered to make an apology and fined £1,500. I felt no personal self-satisfaction that 'I was right'. It was merely a matter of doing the job properly.

A woman complained that she didn't get the land she expected on separation from her husband and blamed counsel. The Court Judgement, which I read, was dead against her and explained she was not a 'compelling witness', which is a nice way of saying she was a liar. Initially, until I'd grappled with a lot more F & B, I had a certain amount of sympathy for her. However, as the exchange of letters between us went on, the holes in her case began to emerge. She was evasive and caught herself out on a number of occasions. I was patient but not fooled. I dismissed her complaint without blaming her but merely stuck to the facts.

In another vitriolic case, the complaint was actually initiated by the wife's father. One could sense what an appalling family upset this all must have been having. The wife's counsel was heard in Court to call the husband a 'tosser'. He probably was but even if provoked, barristers are expected to behave with decorum; a rap over the knuckles coming his way.

There was a Chinese woman living in Canada. She could write no English, so a Canadian friend, whose first language didn't sound to be English either, translated. She didn't like her divorce settlement (I think). Later on she didn't like the Consent Order either. This was even more puzzling as, presumably, she'd signed the document having had it explained to her. I hid behind the 'not in the Bar of England and Wales's jurisdiction' cop out. A bit pathetic (by me) but really the whole problem really lay in Canada. I did advise her to seek legal help there.

There was endless mathematical detail from an ex-husband who did not like paying maintenance. He must have been an accountant. He accused counsel for his ex-wife of misleading Court by manipulating the finances. It was simply beyond me so sent it to a member of the PCC who was admired for his grasp of financial wizardry. The accused barrister, who clearly had more than A Level Maths, got off the hook. The ex-husband was livid.

The 2nd Mrs D complained on behalf of her new husband against counsel for the 1st Mrs D. This was a departure from the norm. I hope Mr D made a good choice in getting rid of the 1st Mrs D for the delights of the 2nd. The actual complaint was woolly and utterly over-emotional, reminding me of Mrs Bucket.

However, maintaining a mental straight face, if you can do that, I went ahead with my F & B. It all really petered out when Mrs D number two, had got it off her chest. She'd shown her mettle and was not to be ridiculed – I think that is what she accused counsel of doing to her new husband, but he didn't have a say in the matter. I dismissed the complaint as kindly as possible.

This was closely followed by a Wing Commander of the Royal Air Force who didn't like the tone of questioning of his wife by counsel for the Respondent. It was quite difficult to unravel as the Wing Co expected considerable deference from lawyers, whom he probably despised, and certainly from the complaints commissioner, whom he probably despised even more, especially if he realised the latter had been in the army, which hopefully he didn't. There was nothing in it except some latent pomposity. So I issued a suitably matching pompous dismissal, taking great care to conceal my former rank and decorations. (The latter are, unattractively, called 'post nominals' in the RAF).

A woman in dire financial straits was a complainant who had lost her house in her divorce, due to some asset valuation which was complicated. She told me, 'I only know that what I wanted, I was not allowed to get'. I did have much sympathy and tried to unravel as much as I could. I was tempted to dismiss it because there was nothing really against the barrister; the unpleasant divorce laws were simply against her. However, to be certain, I passed it to a member of the PCC for advice. A beautifully drafted Opinion was sent back to me, explaining exactly why the complainant had lost her house. I paraphrased it, split the infinitives and sent it to the lady, pretending it was all my own work. Of course, she didn't like it but, hopefully, now understood the situation rather better.

In a child contact case, there was a complaint that counsel had not asked all the questions his client wanted. This was not an isolated situation and I try to explain to complainants that the barrister is a professional and must play the game to the best of his/her ability. This means a selection of what to ask, when. I also tell barristers they must explain the tactics to their client if they can. I went to the barrister, in accordance with my procedure, and sent his response to the complainant. To a certain extent it cleared the air as the barrister was able to explain why he had done what he did. With hindsight he should have done so with his client earlier but in the rough and tumble of the court this is not always possible where he has to think on his feet and react to surprises. I think the complainant understood when I dismissed it but, as in all these things, a divorce is a divorce and people who say it was 'amicable' are, in my view, not 'compelling witnesses'.

There was a complaint against the barrister representing the Child Support Agency (CSA) by a Colonel in the Adjutant General's Corps (an Educator). I didn't know him so there was no conflict of interest. It was, unsurprisingly, very well laid out and needed a matrimonial expert on the PCC to untangle the responsibilities of who did what. In the end, the Colonel had been exasperated, and subsequently defeated, by bureaucracy rather than any fault by the barrister.

The complainant failed in his appeal against the loss of his shotgun licence in his divorce. The Judge clearly recognised the danger signals and, given the detail the barrister disclosed to me, just as well. Reverse of the shotgun marriage? Another didn't like his Iranian ex-wife's concealment of cash. There were no volunteers to go to Iran to help him recover it. Then a divorcee tried to involve us in wriggling out of a divorce financial settlement on account of iffy diplomatic immunity in Austria. All fun while it lasted

A barrister, acting when non-practising, was instructed by his wife, who was a solicitor. There are many barristers who do not have a practising certificate either by choice or because they do not qualify for one. Such barristers used to be called non-practising barristers (now non-registered). Some barristers without practising certificates do provide legal services and are, in effect, practising as lawyers. Even though the rules which apply only to practising barristers do not apply to them, all non-practising barristers remain members of the profession and are expected to conduct themselves in an appropriate manner. In this context, they remain subject to certain rules in the Code of Conduct. If they provide legal services, they have a responsibility not to mislead anyone about their status.

The complaint was initiated by the wife's ex-husband with whom she was in an Employment Tribunal conflict. I was not at all sure whether the barrister was acting legitimately in the first place and therefore what powers the Bar had over him, if any. I thought they probably had. Anyway, given the murkiness of the wife's involvement in the Employment Tribunal, this was well above my pay grade. While this needed a 'cold towel round the head' analysis, it was, ultimately, going straight to the PCC, but in, I hoped, reasonably digestible form.

A divorcee, obtaining a Court Order in her favour, thought all was well. However, the ex-husband went absent and refused to pay up. She now attacked the ex-husband's barrister for allowing this to happen. Gently, I told her that it was not his responsibility to make the husband pay but the Court's. Regretfully, she had to return to Court to enforce payment. In a separate child contact case, in which the solicitors were also complaining, resulted in wasted cost application against the barrister. This is an application against a legal representative whose conduct in proceedings has been shown to be "improper, unreasonable or negligent" to "show cause" why they should not be responsible for the costs incurred as a result of that conduct. This is quite serious. A 'wasted costs' plays into the hands of those who accuse the Bar of being profligate.

A wife maintained that she should have got more on account of being poisoned by organo-phosphate[24] on her husband's farm. The human and animal toxicity of organophosphate pesticides make them a health and environmental concern. Their use was banned in residential areas in 2001, but their agricultural use, as pesticides on fruits and vegetables, is still permitted, as is their use in insect repellent in public spaces such as parks. This was seriously uncharted territory for me and I became a mini-chemical

24. OP$(OH)3$ + ROH → OP$(OH)2(OR)$ + $H2O$ for the chemically inclined readers.

expert after considerable investigation with Counsel and solicitors. It was a good try by the wife but, ultimately, nothing in it. In reaching his conclusion the Judge had clearly accepted the wife's assertion that she had been poisoned and reflected it in the settlement. Nevertheless, it was seriously unpleasant for the wife, whatever the gravity of the poisoning, and I had much sympathy; not something one would want to experience oneself.

In the run up to divorce proceedings, each applicant has to fill in a Form E. A Form E[25] is a standard Statement which both parties will complete with a view to providing each other with a complete picture of their financial position. Clearly, there was room for all sorts of subterfuge and concealment and we had a number of complaints that the opposing barrister was in cahoots with his client. It often took hours of unravelling. Invariably I'd need help from a matrimonial expert on the PCC.

A self-styled 'legal executive', whatever that meant, told me my job. In a brief as possible response I told him exactly what my job was. He went off in a huff. There was then a poisonous separation where the former partner was a woman barrister – hence the aggrieved coming to me to score professional points against her. It didn't work as I could quite clearly see through it.

A dotty woman told me all about the matrimonial rights of women in Austria. It wasn't in the least bit interesting and nothing to do with me. I explained to her what I did in as kind a way as possible. She then wrote another three letters which I answered in shorter and shorter paragraphs each time. Eventually, she got the message, or ran out of stamps. This was closely followed by a whine from a woman who had only secured a 63% settlement of her ex-husband's funds. She'd actually signed the Consent Order so was on a hiding to nothing legally but, she told me in words of one syllable what she thought of the judicial system and, after my dismissal, what she thought of me. For some time afterwards, I had it framed in the downstairs loo. Of course, it should have remained in the Bar's archives but I couldn't resist it.

25. Matrimonial Causes Act 1973.

SEX RAISES ITS UGLY HEAD

A 60 year old man gets rid of his 20 year old Russian 4th wife but doesn't like the deal. This was sad but his friends should have warned him what he was letting himself in for when it was clear she was what is euphemistically called a 'lingerie model'. I sympathised and tried one of my 'old soldier' letters i.e. but for the Grace of God…. I had a hilarious reply, with some intimate detail, which I will not repeat here.

The wife's counsel made homophobic remarks about the husband. It was a child contact case hotly pursued as the husband was now gay. Nevertheless, the barrister should have kept his views to himself. Then a husband was rude about wife's Counsel. Nothing new in that, but in this case, the wife supported her about-to-be ex-husband, which was most certainly new. A rap over the knuckles on its way.

A chap accepted a lump sum agreement, instead of a percentage, two years ago and came to me to have the deal reversed since the percentage would have been better. I fear no chance and explain these things cannot be reversed unless there is some very persuasive new evidence. There was none and he accepted that. A novel one appeared next: a female barrister went on holiday with her client, the husband. The wife didn't like it and gave me some, probably imaginative, detail. It wasn't against the rules; merely a rather more intimate counsel/client conference than normal. I explained this to the wife, trying not to sound like a 'red-top' journalist. I seem to recall the lady barrister was extremely attractive.

A possible conflict of interest arose. Counsel was acting for her lover v. her lover's ex-wife. The complaint was raised by ex-wife's current lover. Try to work it out. On the face of it, it looked uncomfortable, conduct-wise. I took some advice and it came down to the fact that, while not strictly against the rules, the ex-wife's counsel should make something of it in court – ridicule and cynicism? I don't know whether he did or not but the complaint dried up.

Very occasionally there is a typo in the documentation. In this case the husband had to give the wife £317,000 not £17,000 that was in the document. He tried to wriggle out of it, however the law has a neat way of dealing with this called the 'slip rule'. This enables the Court to correct obvious mistakes without going into a long rigmarole.

Tips for Barristers

To end on a slightly happier note, in my talks to barristers in the Family Division, I try to give them advice, hardly as an expert, but from my point of view when a complaint lands on my desk. Hopefully these are the things that they can do to avoid my clutches:

The Courts. Courts are bread and butter to you, but to your client they are terrifying places even in the cosiest Judge's Chambers, and they wish to leave them as quickly as possible hence maybe losing concentration. Ensure your client is listening, and, taking in, what you are saying. If really important points are being made, do the George Bush Snr "Watch My Lips". Human nature being such, we tend to listen to, and read the good bits and skate over the bad. Do not talk 'over' your client to your instructing solicitor. If it is a question addressed to your client allow him/her to respond, not through the solicitor.

Consent Order. If there is any doubt in your mind that your client is being fluffy, get him/her to sign the draft. So often, when the client eventually sees the typed version, they say "I never agreed to that!" Make your solicitor write notes of your discussions with your client or make your own if no solicitor present. They will be invaluable later if a complaint reaches me.

Financial Outcome. Ensure your client knows exactly what the deal is, down to the last penny. It might surprise you how much, in a complaint, I am invited to delve into the minutiae of pension schemes, going rates for house prices, offshore funds and lost winning lottery tickets.

Negotiations. Much of your work, quite properly, will be negotiating with the other side in order to reach agreement where possible. Explain that it is always better to avoid actually going into court if possible. Tell your client what you are doing. If you do not, he/she will think you are in cahoots with the opposing barrister, and probably the Judge. Your client may well think the opposing barrister is telling lies ('misleading the Court'). Explain that counsel acts on instructions; it is not his/her job to scurry around verifying facts. Explain the basis of privilege to your client and what can be legitimately challenged or ignored. If you agree a time/place to meet, stick to it. If there is a transport problem, telephone to explain. Clients are highly stressed and, if you are late, or somewhere else in court, it merely adds another reason for complaining (and sometimes is very difficult to refute).

Child contact. Make absolutely certain that you and your client totally understand each other when negotiating time/place of, say, pick-up; who has the child for how long; Christmas, Easter etc. "Three weeks in the summer holidays" is not the same as "three consecutive weeks" or "the first three weeks of the summer holidays".

Intelligence. All laymen know that barristers are, by definition, very clever. They have to be otherwise they could not be barristers. So you do not have to prove it but you may well have to satisfy your client that you have put sufficient work into their case. Clients are particularly suspicious if you have been instructed late (the original barrister may, for example, be part-heard somewhere else where the case has not concluded) and they cannot imagine how you have had the time to read umpteen lever-arch files.

The Client. Your client will, of course, know their case inside out and may well have firm views as to how you are to run it. Instil confidence, even if you do not feel it. Inevitably there will be different options which, ultimately, your clients must decide themselves. For instance, your client may want more time (to find extra money, to seek different valuations of property). Explain the problems over adjournments and the dangers of wasted costs. Judges have to operate within various parameters. Explain to your client what those are so that they can see the constraints. There are things that are the responsibility of your instructing solicitor. (Clients are, understandably, uncertain about who does what). If you have recommended that, say, in conference or in an Advice, that your solicitor does certain things, ensure your client knows that is what your solicitor must do and, if it is not done, then your client (and probably you) must tackle the solicitor.

Children Act. If we anticipate that a complaint is going to be made that will contain material protected under the Children Act, we warn the complainant. However, this does not always work and clients do not understand. If you can see a problem arising, make sure your client knows that material must be cleared by the Court.

***

So much for that but let me turn to the darker side of man's behaviour. One of the extraordinary things about sex offenders, which I'm in no doubt would be easily answered by psychiatrists, is that they never seem to think they have done anything wrong. Hence their enmity towards barristers, both for and against, and then to me. Having knocked about in the army for some 35 years, I wouldn't have described myself as having led a sheltered life but some of the stuff that came in front of could make even my hair stand on end.

There was a complaint by a rather curious pseudo lawyer against prosecuting counsel for not stopping a rape case. Surely this was up to defending counsel? The courtroom environment in rape cases was fraught with all sorts of difficulties and the police are constantly being blamed by one side or the other. I was simply out of my depth and had to approach a senior member of the PCC for advice. That advice was that the prosecutor was not to blame in a very emotional and convoluted trial.

Then a prisoner, doing nine years on eight charges of indecent assault and three of gross indecency, with others left on the file, sent a very manipulative and evasive complaint. Unsurprisingly, his complaint was that his barrister should have got him off for a number of reasons and, failing that, should have got him a very less severe sentence. All became all too clear after counsel's response to my enquiry, a copy of which I sent to the complainant in dismissing the complaint. I didn't hear back so whether he accepted he was wrong or merely wrote it off, I'll never know. This was followed by a complaint by a paedophile against four

SEX RAISES ITS UGLY HEAD

barristers. I was given the complete story involving Mars bars and self-photography. Not for bedside reading before you put your light out. He had a QC and junior barrister defending him, mirrored by the prosecution. All four came into his sights as being incompetent, vindictive etc etc. So, I had to go to all four for comment. Their replies went to the complainant who then riposted, line by line. This went on for some time until I reckoned it had run its course and dismissed it. Of course, he then went to the LSO. She supported my decision but privately noted my increasing exasperation in the tone of my letters to the complainant. She most certainly would not have enjoyed reading the detail. An enduring aspect of these kinds of sex offenders is that they can never seem to come to terms of what they have done and have no problem in detailing it.

Next there was a complaint against counsel for failing to disclose some evidence when defending a rapist of her eight year old son. The rapist got five years and counsel will respond when he obtains clearance (Children Act) and the prisoner decides whether to appeal or not. Unsatisfactory for the complainant but she understands how slowly the wheels of justice grind. Later there is a re-trial and the mother again complained against counsel for the defendant for allowing it to happen, thereby putting her child through additional trauma. Sickening but I check to see if there is misconduct. I suspect not and that was confirmed by a member of the PCC. The barrister was doing his job, however unpleasant it was. This is one of the horrors of sex offences.

A rapist in Belmarsh Prison would like me to visit him to discuss my dismissal of his complaint, Counsel had responded to the complaint and I'd forwarded it to the prisoner, who had replied. I'd then dismissed it on the grounds that counsel had done his best as far as I could see. There was a further exchange of letters which I showed the barrister who, again, replied. This made no difference. However, I sent the complainant a copy of the barrister's final response, not for comment, but merely to reinforce my decision. The complainant still wanted to see me. I told him that was not something I did; otherwise I'd spend all my time running around the country visiting prisons. He got the point.

There was a 41 count indictment of indecent assault and buggery. The criminal lost his appeal (what a surprise) and came to me. I read the Appeal and was certainly not going to overturn the judge's decision. There was no need for expert advice in this case. Marginally better occurred in a rape/indecency case where the criminal said counsel was good but not great. This was a sort of semi complaint. The rapist was found guilty and accepted his sentence. I did nothing. Another rapist sent me his file eight inches thick with unbelievably revolting detail. Lucky my skin is nearly as thick. The next charmer was guilty of 14 counts of indecency with children. He got ten years. This was a very low sentence. He was lucky not to have it reviewed but I didn't put it that way in my dismissal.

A Muslim got 15 months jail for child beating. However, counsel's response was very thin and further information was required in the light of complainant's reply. Later there were wild accusations of lies and conspiracy by lawyers. It actually went nowhere but counsel should have taken more trouble with his initial, somewhat arrogant, response to me. It went to the PCC who referred it to an Adjudication Panel. An elderly sex offender tried to exonerate himself after a 16 year sentence for rape, incest and buggery. It was all to do with taking shower gels and ointments into public swimming baths; I was not spared the full detail. All appeals were now exhausted so he turned to me. It would be pathetic and sad if it had not been quite so repellent.

A case of sexual violence, procuring prostitution, incest and cruelty appeared. I could do no better than endorse the Appeal Court's clear judgement, so I dismissed it. It was, I have to say, one of the worst examples of human degradation. Another complainant raped a prostitute. Quite clearly, he thought there was nothing wrong in doing so and why therefore, he asked me, was he in prison? It was hardly rape if he'd paid her, was it? OK, there was a bit of violence but that was all part of sex games, wasn't it? Not the sort of violence he meted out I explained to him, with alacrity, in dismissing his complaint.

SEX RAISES ITS UGLY HEAD

I had a submission from the LSO's office, asking if I could edit some of the more revolting sex cases that came across her desk after my conclusion. While I appreciated her sensitivity, I explained that if the complainant found out that I had 'doctored' the file before sending it to her, I'd be in serious trouble. Sorry.

8

Home and Abroad

I DRAFTED THIS CHAPTER DURING the turmoil of replacing a disgraced prime minister of Great Britain and the appalling invasion of Ukraine by Russia in 2022. It starts with my appearance in front of the Wicks Committee.[26] This committee was tasked to delve into the conduct of people in public life and to report to the prime minister, with recommendations for improvement. It then covers my attendance at a symposium in Moscow, with the aim of helping the Russian legal system lurch into the 21st century.

On 28 May 2002, Jonathan Acton Davis QC, chairman of the PCC, and I appeared in front of the Wicks Committee. Never having done this sort thing before and only seen, on television, individuals being grilled by parliamentary select committees, we did some work together before our big day.

We duly appeared in an unimpressive building in Petty France. We sat together in front of Sir Nigel Wicks, who was flanked by senior civil servants. Behind us sat our executive sec-

26. Eighth Report of the Committee on the Standards in Public Life. Chairman Sir Nigel Wicks GCB CVO CBE.

retaries, ready to prompt us at critical points. For Jonathan, a seasoned courtroom Queen's Counsel, used to interrogating witnesses and being on the receiving end of hard questioning, this was, probably, no big deal. However, for me, although experienced in giving presentations and being severely questioned at the various military staff colleges I'd attended, this was something new. I had never faced a formal, and deliberate, investigation into my conduct. While I had nothing to hide, my adrenaline surged. I sought to maintain an air of quiet confidence, which I did not feel. However, we were not under attack but facing genuine, straightforward questioning on what we did and how our process worked. Once under way, my apprehension evaporated.

The Committee on Standards in Public Life was set up in October 1994 by the then prime minister, John Major, against a backdrop of public disquiet. The immediate causes of concern were threefold: (a) the 'cash for questions' scandal involving a small number of Members of Parliament who were alleged to have accepted payment in order to raise questions in the House of Commons; (b) allegations that former ministers were obtaining employment with firms with which they had had connections whilst in office, and (c) a perception that appointments to public bodies were being unduly influenced by party political considerations. In response, the committee was given broad terms of reference: 'To examine current concerns about standards of conduct of all holders of public office...' Within six months, the committee, under the chairmanship of the Rt Hon the Lord Nolan made its first report to the Prime Minister, focusing on MPs, the executive (ministers and the civil service) and public appointments.

While strictly speaking neither Jonathan nor I were publicly appointed, we, nevertheless, clearly had roles directly affecting the public. The Chairman of the Bar saw it, rightly: our place was to give evidence before the committee. In a sense, these sorts of parliamentary committees are an essential part of our democratic fabric. The great and, perhaps, not so good are, sometimes unwillingly, forced to attend. Prime ministers to Silicon Valley technocrats and billionaire bankers are obliged to subject themselves to scrutiny and interrogation by an All-Party group. Refusal to do so can result in contempt of parliament.

Before appearing, we thought it worth reminding ourselves of Nolan's Seven Principles of Public Life.

SEVEN PRINCIPLES OF PUBLIC LIFE

1. **Selflessness.** Holders of public office should act solely in terms of the public interest. They should not do so in order to gain financial or other benefits for themselves, their family or their friends.

2. **Integrity.** Holders of public office should not place themselves under any financial or other obligation to outside individuals or organisations that might seek to influence them in the performance of their official duties.

3. **Objectivity.** In carrying out public business, including making public appointments, awarding contracts, or recommending individuals for rewards and benefits, holders of public office should make choices on merit.

4. **Accountability.** Holders of public office are accountable for their decisions and actions to the public and must submit themselves to whatever scrutiny is appropriate to their office.

5. **Openness.** Holders of public office should be as open as possible about all the decisions and actions that they take. They should give reasons for their decisions and restrict information only when the wider public interest clearly demands.

6. **Honesty.** Holders of public office have a duty to declare any private interests relating to their public duties and to take steps to resolve any conflicts arising in a way that protects the public interest.

7. **Leadership.** Holders of public office should promote and support these principles by leadership and example.

It is worth giving an extract of the Wicks Report in relation to ourselves as it was considered a fairly major element of the Bar's success story in complaint handling.

"When the Lay Commissioner, Major General Michael Scott CB CBE DSO, and Jonathan Acton Davis QC, Chairman of the Professional Conduct and Complaints Committee gave evidence to us, they began with an overall observation about regulatory bodies. They suggested that "it was axiomatic that any regulatory body, whether self- or publicly-regulated, should have on it representation from those who are not part of the profession." They gave three reasons:

• to give public confidence;
• to add a non-professional dimension;
• to prevent development of an incestuous, inward-looking profession.

In describing the role of lay members, they stressed that they should be "impartial and even-handed", not merely "the champion of the consumer or complainant". They must also be self-confident and robust, not shy of stating their opinions. They should be selected by a process involving lay representatives which is open to public scrutiny. Transparency in general was an important feature "in order to give the public the confidence there is no white-wash, cover up or self-protection". The Commissioner's annual report was another aspect of that. The Bar Council has also commissioned an external assessment of how the system is seen to work."

We were very courteously treated and, I think, came out of it with our integrity unblemished.

A place where integrity and morality is not so obvious is Moscow. Putin had become President in March 2000 but had not yet bent the law entirely to his will. There was still hope.

The Lantern Corporation was run by the husband and wife barristers Michele and Christopher Parnell to further the advancement of the Russian legal system. They set up a seminar to be held at the offices of the Federal Securities Commission at Staromonetny Pereulok, Moscow, in September 2000. While handling complaints against lawyers was still a step in the far distance for the Russians, I, together with a clutch of legal luminaries, was asked to speak. I'd never been to Moscow, so this was an excitement. The audience was to comprise representatives from the Federal Commission, the Department for Economic Crimes, the Investigation Department of the Main Directorate of Internal

Affairs, the Regional Department for Organised Crime, the Federal Tax Police Service, the Federal Security Service of the Moscow Region, the Moscow Arbitrage Court and representatives of the enforcement and supervision agencies from the various regions of the Russian Federation. Phew!

We were to be accompanied by our wives, had a very good programme and accommodated in the luxury Marriott Grand Hotel in Tverskaya Street. On arrival at Sheremetyevo Airport, not for us a two hour toil through passport control, as we were immediately swept through VIP facilities. One of the particular joys was that in the party were Paul and Elizabeth Heim. Paul was a highly esteemed barrister. They were old friends of my wife, who had introduced them prior to their marriage. She had met Paul when she lived in Kenya and introduced him to Elizabeth on her return to London in 1964. Arguably, Paul was one of the finest international barristers of his generation.

Paul was born in Vienna in 1932. Following the annexation of Austria by Nazi Germany, life for Jewish people rapidly became challenging. He fled Austria in 1939 with his mother and sister, his father was overseas at the time. Many Jews, who could not leave, including Paul's grandparents and other family members, were murdered by the Nazis. Paul's family travelled first to Cyprus, then Egypt, Israel, and Tanzania, settling in Kenya and later the United Kingdom. Educated first in Nairobi, he read Law at Durham University. Initially returning to Kenya in 1955, he served for 10 years at the Supreme Court in Kenya, before moving to the European Court of Human Rights, the European Parliament, and the European Court of Justice. He was a visiting professor at Leicester University and an honorary research fellow of the University of Exeter. He was made a Grand Officer, Order of Merit of the Duchy of Luxembourg and a Companion of the Order of St Michael and St George. Throughout his life, Paul remained passionate about encouraging young people to reach their full potential and founded several educational awards. He co-founded the Somerset Anne Frank Awards in 2010. Sadly, he died in September 2020 aged 88, followed by Elizabeth in 2022.

SEX RAISES ITS UGLY HEAD

We were very fond of them both. His son is now an eminent barrister.

Building Bridges in European and Human Rights Law: Essays in Honour and Memory of Paul Heim CMG is a unique book, formed as a series of essays in honour of the memory of Paul, the founder of Lincoln's Inn European Group. It focuses on the building of bridges between individuals and institutions in European and human rights law.

The day we arrived, our plane was late and a visit to the Bolshoi theatre had been arranged that first evening, so we were pushed for time. We were asked to assemble at an underground station at a given time, a five minute walk up the road from the hotel to meet everyone. When the Heims and we arrived at the RV we could not see anyone we knew. We hadn't been told there were two entrances to the station and we, inevitably, had the wrong one. We decided the only option was to go by taxi. Paul was fussed about dealing with the taxi driver over the fare. Neither of us spoke Russian and the taxi driver certainly didn't speak English. 'Leave it to me,' I said, being a bit more rough and ready than Paul. I hailed a taxi and asked how much to the Bolshoi. '500 Roubles'. I said, 'Dollars US?' 'Ten'. I held up five fingers, 'Five?' 'OK'. There we were, getting into a taxi, only having just arrived in a communist country, not speaking a word of Russian. We could have been driven anywhere, and never be seen in the land again. We did, however, arrive safely at the theatre.

The programme was tight and talks were to be strictly timed. My heart sank when we were told there would be translation. But not to worry, I was told, it would be instantaneous. I issued a written version of my pitch to the translator, the fluent Sergei, so he could, basically, read it as I spoke. I covered, roughly, the way in which our legal system worked, with solicitors and barristers, then outlined the complaints process. There was no time for questions, so I hoped I hadn't bemused the audience too much. It was difficult to tell from the polite applause. Our accompanying High Court judge was having none of that so, to the Parnells' increasing frustration, went well over time. It was he, at an evening drinks party, who was asked when judges in England ceased to be armed? 'Oh, about 1730, I think'. 'No,' said the Russian, looking at his watch, 'I meant the year, not the time'.

I think we made some sort of progress and the discussions between presentations and at the social gatherings were happy and encouraging. I fear, though, that now, under Putin, this has all been lost.

It was an extremely good visit and we had a certain amount of time to ourselves including dining in a Georgian restaurant and grappling with the Moscow metro system. It always astonished me how my wife was able to identify the stations although, obviously, in Cyrillic writing. The ticket turnstiles were permanently open so being British you wafted through. Unknown to us, you still needed to press your ticket in order for the turnstile to remain open; otherwise it slammed into you with a pelvis breaking thud. Being of an adventurous spirit, and not afraid of very much, my wife had a day off on her own and escaped one of the boring parts of the symposium to travel to the outskirts of Moscow by metro to find the *dacha* of a well known writer.

As she returned to the station, just round the corner, she spotted a funeral and popped into the church to see the open coffin, which was then loaded into a bus-like hearse. She made her excuses and left before any suspicions were aroused from rain-coated, sun-glassed operatives on the fringe of the ceremony. I was glad to see her back.

Keeping to Eastern Europe, we were later visited in London by a delegation of the Board of Advocates of Georgia. While we were flattered and they charming, I'm not absolutely sure what they achieved. It was certainly more than the Iraqi Bar Delegation whose trip was cancelled owing to Baghdad airport being closed while under fire.

But to return to the realities - the lawyers.

9
The Lawyers

WHILE IT IS TIDY TO categorise complaints against barristers into sections such as crime and matrimonial, there are some that don't fit. These can come from solicitors, often a wriggle over fees, or from time to time other complaints made against barristers on a personal basis.

Luckily I never had to involve myself in fee disputes between solicitors and barristers. Barristers, in theory, keep a lofty distance from the filthy lucre but, in reality, kept a very beady eye on their livelihood. Some solicitors would take a chance and come to me with a heavily disguised fee dispute which was easily dismissed. On the whole, I had a very good relationship with solicitors. Most enjoyed working with barristers and were the first to support them against unjustified complaints. In my investigation I therefore set a lot of store by what they said. With the good ones, it was not difficult to detect where, in a solicitor's response to my queries, a barrister was entirely blameless or had gone wrong. However, there was a range of idle, venal, sly, pompous, clapped-out and marginally criminal solicitors with whom I crossed swords. Sadly, I had personal experience, long before I became Complaints Commissioner, with a dishonest solicitor who had fabricated my deceased uncle's will. He went to jail.

Typically, there was a last gasp by solicitors over costs and legal aid funding. Counsel had represented a father, then aged 96 and now deceased, in a financial claim against him by his son. Quite clearly, on the father's death, money had, unsurprisingly, dried up. The solicitors were now scraping the barrel and were trying to recover their losses from the barrister. The barrister had been paid for what he did and no more. Case dismissed. Another solicitor launched a bitter and vindictive complaint against counsel. On investigation I found out that the solicitor was subject to an inquiry by the Law Society. From what my source there said, this was a complete smokescreen so I was able to dismiss without further ado.

A fifth complaint from arrived from Dr P. Dr P is a sort of professional McKenzie Friend but rather liked to think of himself as a lawyer, perhaps a solicitor? Unfortunately, Dr P had a rather higher opinion of his abilities than were actually borne out by the results, usually leading his protégés to their disadvantage. He was not actually a doctor of anything but merely self-styled. He had an agenda of his own relating to *Families Need Fathers*. In 1994, Labour Party MP Glenda Jackson claimed that *Families Need Fathers* advised fathers to kidnap their children if they were not allowed access to them, and if that did not work, to murder the mother. In a subsequent letter regarding the organisation's draft mission statement, she reiterated the kidnapping assertion and found the mission statement to be an *attack on women rather than an argument for keeping children and parents in contact.* In neither instance did the MP provide a source for the kidnapping claim. In 2007, journalist Jenni Murray argued that at its foundation, FNF cast itself outside the frame of respectability as they were said to advocate the abduction of children whose custody was awarded to the mother. To be fair, the organisation is a collection of divorced husbands who think they have been given a raw deal, usually by barristers and the Courts, which sometimes they had. The good doctor saw it as his duty to further litigation by complaining about any barrister who opposed him, which was not a way to further his crusade. While he became a bit of a name to us, each complaint had to be properly investigated just in case there was something in it. There was never a substantiated case against any barrister but it was stressful for them and time-wasting for us.

Later I had a certain amount of bandying of words, after my dismissal, with a forthright man, who had nothing to do with Families Need Fathers but was involved in a poisonous divorce. I'd quietly developed a secret liking for him. He had clearly been hoodwinked by some non-legal nasty bits of work and had some dodgy solicitors in the past but counsel was not to blame. I tried my best to explain why, and it ended on an unusually happy note.

There was a spat in an ethnic minority solicitors' firm. They claimed a non-practising barrister removed some files, probably due to a financial dispute. He denied it, relying on an absence of proof. Apparently the interpreter had them all along. It was really lost in the mist and the solicitors had to prove some sort of misconduct, which they were unable to do. It was interesting in that a non-practising barrister could be employed in a solicitors' firm. I was uncertain whether my writ ran there rather than the Law Society but, luckily, didn't have to face it. In fact, on checking, I did have responsibility.

A solicitors' firm was completely out of its depth in a libel case and their client was advised by counsel to ditch them. It was quite a harsh move and the barrister might have handled it with more grace but did no wrong. In a similar case there was a complaint by solicitors that counsel tried to persuade their client to change solicitors to ones he knew. It happened occasionally when the barrister realised how useless the solicitors were. He was right and perfectly proper to make that recommendation. Sometimes there was client poaching between solicitors, and barristers could find themselves the jam in the sandwich but usually wily enough to latch onto the winning side.

There was a high profile case of a very senior solicitor who had badly fallen out with the hierarchy of the Law Society. It was quite a saga and various barristers were caught up in the process and complained about. As a leading light in the equal opportunities and diversity world, the solicitor wrongly identified me as a possible opponent of her views and demanded to know from our

MINDING THE LAW

executive secretaries if I'd had ethnic minority training. Even with my thick-ish skin, I found it impertinent and offensive, particularly as my esteemed PA's family originated from India and had been chucked out of Uganda by Idi Amin. I looked for an apology, which, of course, failed to materialise. After careful advice from a senior member of the PCC, I was able to dismiss her complaints. Her husband then complained about me to the Chairman of the Bar, who robustly put it where it belonged.

A solicitor didn't like being called 'unprofessional' by counsel. Given the quality of the complaint documentation, I didn't blame the barrister. Likewise, it was probably over the top for a barrister to call a lady solicitor 'Satan's bitch' in court. Ouch. But a rap over the knuckles for both barristers to take more care even if provoked was the result. Another firm was still trying to extract money from a barrister after the matter had been settled by the Bar Mutual Insurance Fund. *Nul points* for a pathetic effort.

My full marks of the year for trying, though, went to the solicitors' firm that sought to extract money they thought owing from a barrister. He was dead. They were infuriated when I explained that the Bar didn't have a compensation scheme for naughty barristers, even dead ones, as here. Compensation could only be paid personally by a barrister. They whizzed off to the LSO, who enjoyed putting them right.

Life was not without its interest though. Solicitors made a complaint against a princess (sic) concubine of a Nigerian chief. Allegedly, she was a barrister, hence their letter to me. I could find no evidence that this lady had been called to the Bar. A sad old man then wrote to me, threatening to firebomb his solicitors. I knew how he felt sometimes but it was not a case for me although I did give him some friendly advice about solicitors taking this sort of threat seriously, so he'd better watch it. There were some stroppy solicitors who complained, but wouldn't reveal whether their client was suing counsel or not. I then received a nice letter from the client disassociating himself from solicitors' letter.

A solicitor appearing in front of the Solicitors' Disciplinary Tribunal didn't like the Law Society's counsel. I bet he didn't,

THE LAWYERS

rather proving counsel was doing his job. Anyway, it would be up to his own defence to take this on, let alone the tribunal chairman if something wrong was happening. I put him in the picture.

Solicitors could annoy me from time to time. It was important, if they were instructing the barrister, to let me have their views in the light of a complaint. Whether they couldn't be bothered, were just idle or thought it beneath them and so didn't respond, irritated me. Sometimes, I wrote personally to the senior partner, conveying a veiled threat that the LSO didn't look kindly on this lack of cooperation. This occasionally galvanised them. Still, one, from whom I had no response for three months despite endless reminders, sent me a blistering letter requiring a reply by return of post. I did so and gave him my, pretty brisk, opinion. Another solicitor's response was important in that counsel was accused of lying. Three letters from us were ignored until I gripped them, giving them 14 days to reply, failing which I was going to the Law Society. They didn't like that and responded with as much bad grace as they could muster.

***

Let me now turn to complaints against barristers which don't fit tidily into the categories I've covered in earlier chapters. These are really against the barrister personally rather than what he/she has done in the course of their work. Sometimes it was what the barrister had or not done in chambers or behaved, publicly, in a manner 'unfitting of the profession'.

A barrister once, jokingly I think, said to me that 90% of barristers were stressed. 'And the other 10%?' 'Very stressed.' Occasionally, this came to me when something had happened in chambers or in court where a barrister flipped. My view was this was inappropriate to be dealt with through the complaints system but better handled sensitively by the barrister's head of chambers. The few cases when this did happen, it usually worked. It is quite proper that stringent rules are made to govern the operation of a system and institution. However, there are times when the rule has to be 'adjusted' in the light of commonsense, compromise and humanity. In my final job in the army, I dealt with promotions and appointments of officers. There were very good rules governing both but, on very few occasions, these had to be adapted. For instance, an officer in the Special Forces had failed to attain the right qualifications for promotion simply because he had been fighting the enemy in the jungle. With the agreement of the promotion board his name went forward for review. (He didn't make it but was grateful for the chance he would not otherwise have had). Very, very occasionally this happened in the Bar. One instance was the case of a barrister who, quite clearly, suffered a nervous breakdown and trashed equipment in his chambers. His behaviour came to me since he could not continue to practise under the circumstances. It was not one for the PCC but a sensible informal arrangement was made with head of chambers until the individual was well enough to resume his work. I did keep the chairman of the PCC informed of what I was doing.

There was a nightmare of a case involving an Indian against counsel, who was also an Indian and spent much time in India. It involved an enforcement order for security of costs. As this was well above my pay grade, I sought, and received, robust advice from a member of the PCC and, accordingly, dismissed the complaint. When is a conditional discharge a conviction, I was asked by a potential complainant? All a bit woolly but counsel faced an adjudication panel for failing to make it clear to his client. He didn't, perhaps understandably, like me telling him what the law was. (I had, of course, quoted directly from the PCC member's note).

I made it an early rule that, on the whole, a complaint by one barrister against another went straight to the PCC without touching the sides. It happened very seldom but when it did it was particularly nasty, usually from rather inadequate individuals. As an interesting aside, I was advised that barristers employed by the Immigration Service had to be dealt with 'in-house' unless the offence was particularly heinous then it would come to me. I don't actually remember any.

Counsel was drunk, leading to his de-instruction by his solicitors who are now, rightly, pursuing him for negligence relating to costs. Not the sort of thing the Bar likes, so straight to the PCC and subsequent Disciplinary Tribunal. There was then an amazing spat between a loopy Ghanaian woman and a Ghanaian barrister. There was nothing in it but counsel had been extremely idle in failing to respond to my letters, so he went to the PCC as well.

Counsel was involved in a traffic accident and did not behave particularly well afterwards, however no misconduct. The solicitors, in the subsequent civil court case, tried to enhance their position by complaining of the barrister's conduct after the crash. It was entirely a matter for the court and I told them so.

I had a complaint from a mad woman all about pensions. Counsel was, in her opinion:
• A filthy lying criminal.
• A professional perjurer.
• A drug-soaked Zombie.

Brightens my little day. But enhanced with more faxes from Mr P who wants counsel hung, drawn and quartered.

A solicitor involved in the Marchioness/Bowbell Inquiry had been annotated in the report as a 'para-legal' by counsel. She resented this and accused him of libel. A woman scorned. While hardly misconduct, the sensible way out for everyone was for him to apologise. He did.

Some Chambers problems. Unusually, for some reason, I had to write to a head of chambers. He failed to reply to four letters of mine. So, I'm afraid, an automatic referral to PCC. In another case involving chambers, counsel failed to turn up for an Asylum Appeal tribunal. Both instructing solicitors and chambers' clerks had made a diary nonsense. Head of chambers took the rap, apologised and the complainants gracefully withdraw. Occasionally there were sex discrimination allegations by barristers against heads of chambers; basically because they hadn't been given the jobs by the clerks they thought they ought to on account of their sex i.e. female. The Bar Council has tried to stamp this out but it goes on, sometimes in the mind of the complainant but, anyway, not something for me but straight to PCC. Related to it are unpleasant sex advances to pupils. 'Come to bed with me and I'll see you OK in chambers' or words to that effect. The Bar Council was taking severe steps to eradicate this problem. There was a barrister well-known for rather futile fumbling, who was swiftly rebuffed for his efforts. He had a very apt nickname which I am not brave enough to reveal here. A dishonest barrister was sacked from chambers. The other barristers in chambers complained. It should never have come anywhere near me being entirely a chambers problem to sort out. An iffy barrister tried to get me to investigate chambers when civil proceedings against him were *en train*. Nothing doing; he should have known better. Not brilliant for his future. Head of chambers tried to use me to get at counsel for non-payment of rent. Your problem, not mine. A woman claimed she was owed money by chambers but didn't know how much. Not very helpful. I could hardly progress without knowing the detail.

There was a complaint of bad language on the telephone to a scam operator (£1 a minute) but the caller should not have said she was a barrister. I don't deal with scammers and, in terms of bad language, he fully deserved what he got but, nevertheless, the barrister should not have 'threatened' by using the word 'barrister' in that context. I dismissed with politer language than I felt.

In the courts. A police officer claimed counsel frightened him. Unusual I would have thought and it didn't sound quite right. Details were too vague even to investigate. This was not the same police officer who complained that counsel was drunk and therefore 'wasted police time'. Readers might remember the well-publicised arrest of the man who gave the police horse a sausage roll, 'because he looked hungry.' The story, sadly, does not relate which barrister managed to keep a straight face in the subsequent court case. A complainant demanded I obtain tapes from Court so I can hear counsel sniggering. No. A barrister was accused of vilifying a litigant-in-person opponent. Barristers find these people very irritating and frustrating and, occasionally lose their *sang-froid*. To the PCC for a low level rap over the knuckles. Another made inappropriate remarks in court with regard to a dyslexic, agoraphobic, claustrophobic litigant-in-person. Another called a litigant-in-person a vexatious litigant when he wasn't. Straight to the PCC for both, then Summary Hearings. A judge complained that counsel's cross-examination was conducted in such a way as to cause the jury to be discharged. This was extremely serious resulting in all sorts of financial mayhem. Not at all good for the barrister's future. Rather less important but acutely embarrassing was when prosecuting counsel had his file stolen by the defendant. You mustn't laugh. There was a complaint by a judge claiming that a barrister had referred to 'in-camera' matters in public. This was very serious and it went straight to a disciplinary tribunal via the PCC. A highly sensitive German woman heard a mock accent by opposing counsel. 'Do not talk about die Var.' She later accepted a profuse apology. In a separate case, Mr S was satisfied with my decision but remarked that that judge was gay. Utterly irrelevant but he was right.

Occasionally the race card came into play and inevitably went to the PCC. Counsel made a racist remark to a magistrate's clerk. Unprintable here. In a separate case a Muslim barrister was rude about Jewish ones. These things were a real shame because, certainly, in my view, the Bar was very 'inclusive and diverse' and everyone, whatever background or origin, seemed to get on happily together.

A barrister failed to obey a court order to pay the complainant £14,000. This is a clear breach of the Code of Conduct. If anyone, a barrister must comply with the law. Counsel called a witness a 'waster' and 'jobsworth'. He may well have been right, but barristers cannot say things like that and especially one who called the judge a 'robot'. Summary Hearings via the PCC. A woman complained against three barristers for making her husband appear in court when ill. He subsequently died. It was very difficult to deal with sensitively because the barristers were doing their job properly but it certainly didn't look like that to her. It was really up to the judge. A disabled police officer suffered panic/anxiety attacks from rude counsel. Clearly there was a useless judge, who should have gripped what was happening in his court.

MINDING THE LAW

Unusually, there was a complaint by a judge against a bumptious woman barrister. Normally, judges happily dealt with this sort of thing themselves without bothering to come to me. Occasionally though, they want the barrister's 'card' marked rather than just a bollocking in court.

Overseas cases were always interesting because I was not always sure the Bar Council had jurisdiction and often had to seek advice unless it was blatantly obvious one way or another. There was, for instance, a complaint by a Cayman Islands judge against a barrister over, I think, money laundering. Interesting merely because of the provenance and detail. We did have jurisdiction although I was rather hoping I'd be required to visit the Cayman Islands to check. Counsel was accused of not replying to UN genocide crime people in Arusha. Solved by giving him a fierce telephone call to get a move on. Dormant counsel working in New York. Lovely word; does it really mean 'asleep'? Certainly not in our jurisdiction. Mr G, living in Australia, complained about his brother, a barrister in Singapore. I reckoned we had jurisdiction as he had been called to the Bar in England. *He* clearly didn't as he refused to reply to my letters. It was to 'lie on the file' as they say in police circles to the dissatisfaction of the brother. An Italian lawyer complained about a barrister working for a solicitors' firm in Grenada, West Indies, and there was a complaint about a fee by an Austrian against a Turkish barrister in Cyprus. Both out of jurisdiction. Corruption in high places concerned a non-practising barrister in Bangladesh who was a minister of something. Luckily not for me. There was a complaint from Rawalpindi Bar Association about a barrister advertising. Barristers are not allowed to advertise but I don't have jurisdiction in the subcontinent. I extracted the relevant part of the Code of Conduct and let them have a copy.

A couple of pro bono complaints. A 'traveller' was whining about paying council tax. He complained against a barrister, who was representing him for free. Some people are never satisfied; a disgraceful complaint. I advised another complainant, who alleged counsel said 'pro bono' but is now charging, to seek urgent solicitors' help.

People would sometimes complain against members of boards or institutions for reasons totally unconnected to the law but, when they discovered the object of their wrath was a barrister, they used our process, usually without success. For example a barrister would not write a reference for an ethnic minority potential solicitor. Given his English, I'm not surprised. In another case a ludicrous man, who failed to get a vacancy on a law course, blamed a member of the staff of the course as he was a qualified barrister. There was a complaint against a university law professor but before he became a barrister, so no chance. There were seven complaints against the head of Professional Conduct of Royal College of Veterinary Surgeons since he was a barrister by trade. I'm afraid this is one for the vets to handle themselves. A sacked male nurse sought to have a go at counsel employed by Royal College of Nursing. Certainly a matter for the college, not me. All of these I was able to dismiss without fussing a member of the PCC.

Occasionally, exasperated members of the public, trying to obtain what they thought they were owed by a barrister, would come to me. For instance, allegedly counsel failed to pay his house cleaners but this was hardly a matter of legal misconduct. I reminded the complainant of the small claims court facility. A barrister left a flat owing rent and costs of dilapidations. The owner complained to me but it was really one for the civil court. Why not merely withhold the deposit? There was a possible conflict of interest in that the complainant was suing a building firm that had done work for counsel. No, the barrister was not involved in this litigation and therefore had nothing to do with the complaints procedure against barristers. Counsel dropped out of buying a house. I could easily see the exasperation and disappointment but not one for me. However, there was a claim that money had been given to a barrister, who denied it. Photographs of cleared cheques were then produced. This was, essentially, a civil matter but the barrister had behaved badly, so went to the PCC for a subsequent summary hearing. Another was getting nowhere in a dispute with his bank, so has a go at counsel employed by the bank. Clever of him to find this out but not one for me.

Have you ever pressed 'send' on an email and, later, realise it has gone to the wrong person? Barristers are not immune. I had a complaint that counsel working in a solicitors' office inadvertently sent an email to their client saying he is an idiot. Loosely coupled with that, solicitors didn't like counsel's letter in the Law Society Gazette personally criticising their firm. Probably right. However, the barrister must show he was right. Another thought counsel's letter to *The Times* incited speeding. Sadly, I no longer have a copy of the letter but it generated considerable ribaldry in my office, particularly when I told a barrister who had chambers in London and Bristol. He was consequently always whizzing down the M4, usually late. On his dashboard he had a yellow Post It note with a large '9' on it. This was to remind him he already had 6 speeding points on his licence and a further 3 spelled 'off the road'. I fear he was well beyond attending the National Driver Offender Retraining Scheme course, which was only available to first time speed merchants to avoid points on their licence. This organisation was otherwise known as 'Speedy Motors'[27] in my family, who had some experience.

The cab rank rule means a barrister must take a case that is within their knowledge and expertise provided they are free to do so, no matter how unpalatable it is. A recent independent report showed the rule protected the interests of the consumer, not the barrister. Here, counsel would not take a case concerning a gay individual and another didn't want to defend a League Against Cruel Sports man. Both are obliged to do so under this very good rule which prevents barristers 'cherry picking' the things they like or don't like.

Some barristers, probably a bit too pleased with themselves, can be over loud or bombastic in public, particularly outside the court rooms in the public arena. In our Victorian built courts,

27. In the The No. 1 Ladies' Detective Agency series of novels by Alexander McCall Smith, Mma Precious Ramotswe's eventual husband is Mr J. L. B. Matekoni, who runs Speedy Motors.

there is seldom a private space for client/lawyer conferences, so these things happen in corners or corridors. They are easily overheard, of course, by people who shouldn't. It also made it simple for the other side to complain. I warn aspiring barrister of this. But there was no excuse for a rude and threatening barrister saying, 'I'm a lawyer' to hospital staff. Utterly unacceptable; straight to the PCC.

But I must leave you with this gem:

'Members of the jury,' counsel said. 'I would like you to dive into the deep blue pool of my mind, where, in the limpid waters, all will be made clear and all difficulties will be resolved.'

'Mr Pakenham,[28] that's quite enough about your swimming pool,' said the judge. 'Could you please arrange to emerge from it.'

'I must ask your lordship to remember that you are merely the pool attendant.'

28. The Hon Patrick Pakenham 1937-2005. A well loved barrister who died much too soon.

10

In Court

I HAD A NUMBER OF CROSSES to bear but none more so than Mr X. He was well up in the rankings of extremely unpleasant complainants. In fact, on a scale of one to ten, he was about 15. X complained of somewhere between nine and twelve barristers, none of whom was to blame for anything. As a consequence of my consistent dismissals, he turned his venom onto me. Over time I received many letters couched in obscene and revolting language. For example, "Only an accomplished motherfucker like yourself could maintain such a duplicitous charade/façade. Bisexual paedophile vermin like yourself are best advised to jump off the top of Northumberland House forthwith." When this had little effect, he sprayed our office outside walls with "Scott is a paedophile." "M Scott pimp," and similar words. The police were after him but despite, on one occasion, his arrest in Lincoln's Inn Field with a rucksack full of spray cans, they couldn't pin it on him. However, not to be put off he took proceedings against me for a 'lack of duty of care'. I had to appear in the Central London County Court in Regent's Park. The case was set for 2 pm on Friday 7 December 2001. This was tiresome as my wife and I had been invited to a cocktail party, and to stay for supper and the night, with some friends near Andover. I was not looking forward to the Friday night exodus from

IN COURT

London in the rush hour traffic, so hoped the case would be over quickly. This was not to be. The problem was that the judge listed to hear the case, at the last minute, had to step down as he had been on the panel that selected me for the Complaints Commissioner's post. Even knowing me that slightly meant that he was 'professionally embarrassed' and could not be seen to be impartial.

Finding a spare judge in London on a Friday afternoon was understandably difficult. Things were not looking good but an hour or so later one was found and the case proceeded. I was defended by Geoff Weddell, an excellent member of the PCC. We'd had a conference before, of course, to discuss it but he appeared in court with a very thick lever-arch binder. I expressed surprise in that, to me, it was open and shut and there was no question of my having any duty of care for the revolting Mr X. However, Geoff said, 'Mike, you are experienced enough now to know what we call 'legal risk'. However confident you might feel something can always go wrong. If, for instance, the judge does think you *do* have a duty of care then I shall show how well you applied it to X.' Sensibly, the judge flung it out and I appeared home to a frantic wife who thought I'd been jailed. We arrived at the cocktail party as people were leaving but luckily in time for dinner and to stay the night.

The X saga doesn't, though, finish there. He was put on the list of vexatious litigants on 23 March 2003 having after being made subject to a Grepe v Loam order in 2002, and was refused permission to sue the Lord Chancellor's department for false imprisonment and contempt of court. Earlier I was asked for evidence to put to the Treasury solicitor for X to be made a vexatious litigant relating to a condom he had sent me in one of his many vitriolic letters. X threatened me with the High Court but offered me a Part 36 offer of £15,000 payable to him – if not, he will claim against me. This didn't stop him vandalising the door to our offices over a weekend.

However, eventually, he got his just deserts by being imprisoned later on a charge unknown to me. I even had a letter from him when he was in HMP Wandsworth. I don't recall the content but it certainly wasn't 'With love and best wishes'.

Another, rather more serious, event was my appearance in the High Court for contempt of court. Technically, civil contempt refers to conduct which is not in itself a crime but which is punishable by the court in order to ensure that its orders are observed. Civil contempt is usually raised by one of the parties to the proceedings. Although the penalty for a civil contempt contains a punitive element, its primary purpose is coercion of compliance. A person who commits that type of contempt does not acquire a criminal record and it is not a criminal offence, even if committed in connection with a criminal case. Examples of civil contempt include disobedience of a court or undertaking by someone involved in litigation, and proceedings will normally be commenced by the other party aggrieved by it.

Early on in my time, I dealt with a complaint by a woman against a barrister, who happened to be her ex-husband. This was a standard ploy to get at a husband/wife in the furtherance of divorce proceedings as I've shown in earlier chapters. I should have been warned by the staff at the Bar Council of the provisions of the Children Act 1989. This, quite rightly, forbade anyone seeing papers relating to a child without permission of the Court. In my innocence, as per my standard procedure, I passed the papers of the complaint to the barrister for comment. Of course, they contained considerable detail of the child in question, a 5 year-old boy, who was the subject of bitter dispute in the divorce. The barrister was apoplectic as well he might be and arranged for me to answer a case of contempt for infringing the Children Act.

I was defended by a lady barrister from the PCC who took it extremely seriously in that conviction could result in a prison sentence. I was fairly confident that this wouldn't happen but, nevertheless, milling around in the corridors of the High Court, my adrenaline mildly surged. This was not helped by Adrian Turner, a good friend and one of the executive secretaries who worked with me, saying, 'It's OK, Mike, we've got the cake'. 'What cake?' 'The cake with the file in it in case you go to HMP Belmarsh'. Wonderfully lightening the mood and raising my morale.

IN COURT

As I took my place in court, in front of Mr Justice Cazalet,[29] my barrister said, 'Mike, you'll sit behind me. When the judge addresses you, stand over to my right so he can see you. He doesn't really like women barristers, so he'll directly talk to you but don't reply, I'll do that'.

The ex-husband barrister was there, eying me with distaste. He was, no doubt, hoping I'd progress swiftly to the slammer. However, all was well and commonsense prevailed. I received a mild rebuke from the judge and was told to send all the papers back to the wife, who had to seek permission from the original court, where her case was being heard, to allow me to see them. It was a severe lesson and from then on, any complaint involving a barrister in divorce went straight to a matrimonial expert on the PCC, without touching the sides.

You might think this would put me off courts but completely the opposite. I very much enjoyed calling in on the criminal courts such as the Old Bailey, officially the Central Criminal Court, and Southwark Crown Court. It was free theatre; no wonder so many barristers were members of the Garrick Club, famously an elite watering-hole for actors. I justified my visits to the courts by telling my colleagues, and myself, that it was good to see the people, about whom I had to read so much, actually in action. The key person I made a beeline for was the Listing Officer, not a person most people have ever heard of but one of the most powerful in the court system. It is the Listing Officer who decides which judge sits in which court over what case. The judges think they rule the courts but it is actually the Listing Officer. I would go to their office and look at the board on which the cases were shown, and in which court they were being held. I'd be briefed on the interesting ones and what stage they had reached. Then, not for me the public gallery, but escorted to a seat in the well of the court where I was close to the barristers. My business card was put before the judge.

29. A High Court judge and an authority on P. G. Wodehouse. He is the principal trustee of Wodehouse's estate, and in 2016, was "delighted" when the British Library acquired the Wodehouse archive in 2016.

By sheer chance, the highlight of these visits was the trial in the Old Bailey of Messrs Korkolis, Zografos, both Greeks, and two Frenchmen, Mereu and Moussaoui. They were charged with kidnap, false imprisonment and blackmail of a Greek shipping agent, George Fraghistas. The full story of the trial is told by one of the jurors, Trevor Grove, in his excellent book *The Juryman's Tale.*[30]

On 24 March 1996, George Fraghistas, after parking in a London NCP car park, was bundled into the boot of a car at pistol point by three masked men. After a short journey, he was hauled out of the boot, a blanket thrown over his head and locked in a cupboard in a nearby mews house. He was blindfolded, hand-cuffed, his ankles bound and earplugs stuffed into his ears. The next day he was forced to make ransom calls to his family. Nine days later he was rescued by the police and the gangsters arrested.

The case was prosecuted by the elegant Joanna Korner QC[31] and each of the defendants had their own counsel, apart from Korkolis who, I think, had dispensed with his early on. I went to the Old Bailey on the 54th day of the trial and was recommended by the Listing Officer to listen to this one. When I arrived, Zografos, the number two bandit, was in the dock being cross-examined by his counsel, Patrick Curran QC. Zografos had a fairly smooth patter that the whole thing was a put-up job by the impoverished Mr Fraghistas to extract money from his family. It was then Mr David Owen Thomas QC's turn. He was Moussaoui's counsel. To my eyes, he was straight out of central casting for *Rumpole of the Bailey*; immaculate, with a gold watch chain across an ample waistcoated tummy. In his book, Trevor Grove recalls that, for some unexplained reason Thomas wanted to know if his client and Mr Mereu (a wrestler) did press-ups and 'other unpleasant things of that kind that went on in the army'. 'They jogged,' Zografos replied. 'You can do too many exercises without special equipment.' 'I think Mr Zografos means you can do a *great* many exercises without equipment – though for me it *would* be too many,' Mr Thomas remarked to the general hilarity of the

30. Bloomsbury 1998.
31. Now a Judge of the International Criminal Court.

court. My memory of this exchange is slightly different. When asked the question, Zografos replied, 'They was on the weights'. 'I think the court will need an explanation here,' said Mr Thomas, 'being 'on the weights' means exercising with dumbbells and gymnastic apparatus etc. Not something, ladies and gentlemen of the jury, you can see me doing'. Much laughter.

I did, however, sail, unintentionally, sometimes a bit too close to the wind.

11
Sailing
close to
the Wind

INITIALLY, I THOUGHT I WOULD be able to do more by conciliation. Apart from the fact that, by the time the complaint reached me, conciliation was far from the complainant's mind, I found myself becoming too involved in the case. One of my attempts went disastrously wrong.

A woman, who worked for an international organisation based in Switzerland, made a complaint. She clearly suffered from some sort of nervous affliction which meant she could only correspond with us by telephone. You will see the difficulty this entails when we, and the barristers involved, have to have things properly recorded on paper. Our secretaries struggled on with this lady who had a very low tolerance threshold over international telephone lines. It was extraordinarily difficult to help her. In the notes on the file were the names and contacts of three of her doctors. With all the proper regard to patient confidentiality, we contacted one of the doctors to try to see if he could help.

Not unnaturally, he had to refer to his patient before responding. When she heard this, she was incandescent with rage and quoted a stricture, which she had previously given us that on no account were any of her doctors to be contacted. (Why she had, in the first place, given us their names, she didn't explain). Anyway, deep down in the file there was the note supporting what she had said. We were extremely embarrassed and sent her our apologies, with flowers, which she rejected. Rightly, I suppose, we were fined. Her series of complaints, which were extraordinarily difficult to understand, fizzled out, much to our relief.

A happier occasion concerned a lady whose new house on a modern estate had been appallingly built by a big construction firm. She sued and was advised by her barrister to accept an out of court settlement. She did not like it and she and I became immersed in correspondence over the detail of her case and, of course, the inadequacies of her house. I had enormous sympathy but the barrister was correct. I explained why and she accepted it with such good grace that she sent me a Christmas card every year. Another time, I desperately tried to persuade a lady barrister to apologise to a complainant for *inadvertently upsetting* her, not to *apologise for the action* she, rightly, took in court. Barristers are apt to think that saying 'sorry' is an admission of guilt which, of course, it sometimes is. In this case, though, I knew it would solve the problem. The barrister simply could not see it and complained about me to her Head of Chambers. After an irate (one-sided) telephone conversation with me, he reported me to the Chairman of the Bar. The barrister subsequently followed my advice to the satisfaction of the complainant.

Another idea I had was to have a sandwich and wine working lunch in my office. I thought this might go, in some way, to show, publicly, that we did care and did have a genuine desire to deal fairly with both complainants and barristers. Perhaps it would spread by word of mouth rather than just on paper. My guests would be a complainant who had 'won' against a barrister, one who had 'lost', and a lay representative and barrister from the PCC. It was a good idea in principle but a nightmare to arrange.

Who to choose from the complainants? The one who had lost would have to be reasonable without the usual venom. (Initially, I fastened on the man who had sent me the tin of corned beef but, when asked, he sheepishly had to admit that his friend had written his complaint and he didn't think it was right to attend. I agreed). After a number of false starts and some unwarranted vitriol, it did work but not something I ever did again.

Neighbourhood disputes featured extensively and it was difficult not to become personally involved because they were easy to understand compared with, say, tricky matrimonial legalities. I had to be careful to curb my natural emotional reaction to people who appeared invariably to damage their lives, financially and psychologically, in their disputes. The barrister's job, in most of these sorts of cases, is to try to persuade their clients to settle out of court. It's almost a failure to have to go into court, which, of course, increases expense and the risk of not only losing but paying their opponents' legal fees. But, no, they want their day in court. In most cases the barrister has done nothing wrong but their client has lost and the anger then turns on them.

For example, one appalling case involved something relatively trivial; parking badly on a shared drive. The complainants poured money after money into their case, eventually having to sell their house and live in a small rented cottage in Wales. I could see how it went wrong and was aghast at how they had virtually bankrupted themselves. But the barrister was not to blame. He saw the case very clearly and the absolute law of who could do what in the drive. There was another long running saga over a village green. A local society managed it but others in the village didn't like their decisions. Argument became impossible to solve so lawyers were instructed. It all became hideously expensive and everyone lost, except the lawyers. There was nothing I could do for them: the villagers, not the lawyers.

Rights of way and boundary disputes were legion. I inwardly groaned when I saw yet another one. I knew, practically before finishing reading the first page of the file, that this was not going to have a happy ending. Coupled with those were people who encroached, sometimes by mere inches, with their sheds, fences or buildings on someone else's land. One chap built a house on land not belonging to him, then didn't like counsel's advice that he didn't have a case against the conveyancer. Again, it was utterly clear, even to a non-lawyer such as me, where the rights and wrongs lay. Another built a garage on his neighbour's land: an absolute classic of a man chancing his arm and then trying again by complaining against the barrister. This sometimes lurched into rows with the local council over planning permission where the builder defied the prohibition in the hope that he'd obtain retrospective permission. Hard-nosed councils don't do that, so he had no leg to stand on and had to demolish. Ouch, but I didn't really have much sympathy.

Then there was the mad Miss M, who was well-known to us. This time she was complaining against Mr L, a barrister. Her original problem was over a relatively trivial maintenance charge on her flat. Because of her endless litigation, and therefore costs, she had lost one flat and was in danger of losing another. She flooded everyone with countless faxes of impenetrable English. She appeared to live with a Dr G who was nearly made a vexatious litigant in another case. What a pair. I dismissed without having to bother the PCC but had no doubt whatsoever that it was bound for the LSO.

The case of the septic tanks in the Turks & Caicos Islands brightened my day. It had the makings of a crime novel but, sadly, was out of my jurisdiction otherwise a visit would have been mandatory. Not far away was a complainant trying to recover money or half share in a house which he had lost to a Scientology freak. He complained against counsel's advice but didn't tell me what it was, so I was powerless to help.

There was litigation against the Forestry Commission over the provision of 'polytunnels'. I'm ashamed to admit I had to find out what a 'polytunnel' was. I'd led a sheltered life when it came to horticulture. Nevertheless, once I grasped the nettle (sorry) I could see that the barrister did have something to answer for, so off to a green-fingered member of the PCC.

Flats and tenancies raised problems. Two brothers were taking on a third over a tenancy. However, they were not showing me the papers. I suspect the solicitors have them and are holding onto them pending payment. There was nothing I could do without, at least, being provided with the relevant documents. There was a Residents Association problem but maybe counsel overstepped the mark by signing himself 'barrister' when it was irrelevant and clearly designed to intimidate, so it went to the PCC. In a separate case, we were trying to be used by a client and his solicitors to have counsel evicted and pay outstanding rent. Counsel was clearly not blameless but it was a civil dispute and nothing to do with the complaints system. The solicitors should have been well up to handling it through the lower courts. A flat owner complained that counsel had failed to act adequately in a dispute with another flat owner in the same block who had carried out inappropriate repairs. There was something in this, so I approached a member of the PCC for advice. My adviser wasn't entirely happy but there was simply not enough evidence to have the barrister before any of our panels, so a reluctant dismissal with some helpful wording from my adviser.

After a particularly gruelling day, I returned to my wife and said if we ever have a row with our neighbours (on one side a highly regarded, well-known playwright and on the other a genial retired High Court judge, so unlikely) we are NEVER to go to Court.

Often, I felt genuinely sorry for a complainant who had, perhaps, been let down by the system, and I became the last resort. They could feel wronged by the law and the process, and the barrister was just part of that, so must in their eyes be in some way to blame. On the whole, barristers could look after themselves and know perfectly well whether they have chanced their arm or cut a corner. Most knew that ethics was not a small county east of London. However, there were those who were hounded by a difficult client or subjected to some clever tactic by an opposing solicitor. Members of the public who thought a barrister's life began at ten am by alighting from the Rolls and gently easing to a large lunch at the Garrick, should have seen the serious financial difficulties many faced at the unglamorous end of, say, magistrates' courts and the like. Some of the explanations for failure to pay practising certificates were illuminating and distressing. These certificates, and I quote verbatim, required the barrister to:

- update any personal details
- verify practising details
- declare the appropriate income band for the purposes of setting the appropriate fee
- update insurance information
- declare practice area information
- make the declarations required for Youth Court work and the Money Laundering Terrorist Financing and Transfer of Funds (Information on the Payer) Regulations and immigration supervision;
- make a declaration of truth
- select optional fees, make payment or delegate authority for payment.

Not for the shy and retiring.

However, I believed wholeheartedly that the disciplinary system of the Bar was very strong. Having been in a Foot Guards regiment, I know what I am talking about. The Code of Conduct had a remorseless grip which was thoroughly endorsed by the PCC. There were no pussycats amongst its members and an outsider would have been astonished to see, sometimes, how the lay members found themselves even *defending* the barrister.

There was nothing in the rules, though, that stopped complainants transfixing me with a laser beam.

12

Up Front and Personal

ONCE I HAD DISMISSED A complaint, you might have thought that that would be the end of it. Not a bit of it. The next step for a complainant would be to approach the LSO. Having done so, even after the LSO's dismissal, the venom would then be re-circulated back onto me. If the LSO criticised me, which happened *very* occasionally, the opprobrium was triumphant.

I was threatened with:

• Police arrest
• Having proceedings taken against me in court.
• Arraigned for contempt in the High Court.
• Subjected to judicial review.
• Put in front of the European Court of Human Rights.
• Issued with a 'picketing notice' (sic) by the Council for Ethnic Minority.
• Reported to the Press Complaints Commission.

UP FRONT AND PERSONAL

Mr Y was involved in a poisonous divorce in which his child was subjected to a bitter tug-of-war. Nothing new here but the emotional self-destruction was appalling. Having learnt my lesson earlier, I was having nothing to do with the papers regarding the child. Mr Y did not like them being returned unread, even after I explained why. He discovered I'd served in the army. It then took on a different hue as my background and record was not difficult to research. So I then became the butt of Mr Y's views on the inadequacy of the officer corps and my part in it. I suspect rather more to his satisfaction than mine.

A very senior barrister, indeed a member of the Bar Council, made an extraordinary after-lunch speech to an assembly of internationally high-powered women, those with heads and shoulders well and truly through the glass ceiling. It contained a series of off-colour jokes, verging on racist remarks, couched in pompous self-aggrandising language, to such an extent that some attendees got up and left while he was talking. The lady running the event complained to me, not so much in the normal vitriolic manner of most complaints but very measured, almost in terms of bewilderment. As was my custom, I sent the complaint to the barrister asking for his comments. I didn't hear from him until I received a call from the Chairman of the Bar. He told me he had met the barrister concerned, in passing, in Chancery Lane, who asked him who this Scott fellow was? The Chairman explained and asked me to give the barrister a call. I did so and told him had it been an entirely private affair, it would have had nothing to do with me, but on the menu, in big bold lettering was his name and subtitle as "Barrister at Law". I told him the procedure of complaints handling, of which he affected to know nothing (fair enough, he was so senior he was above worrying himself with this sort of minutiae). After a bit more of his huffing I started to lose a little of my well-known tolerance and told him that if this wasn't handled sensibly and properly with due regard to the hurt feelings of the ladies, he could easily find himself on the front pages of the *Sun* and *Mirror* – I let my imagination roam over some of the more lurid headlines. He saw the point; it went to the PCC, which arranged for a severe rap over the knuckles. The lady in question was satisfied with this outcome. Happily for us both he avoided me at subsequent Bar Council meetings.

Closer to home, a former officer in my regiment discovered what I did. I was also President of the Third Guards Club, the officers' dining club of the Scots Guards. This made him even more excited. He, with a small coterie of friends, had lost a lot of money in Lloyds. They took proceedings and had a bad time in court owing, in their view, to the inadequacy of their counsel. I explained to him that, effectively, barristers were immune for what they did in court in terms of inadequacy.[32]

(The amended rules of Inadequate Professional Service had not yet come into force but, even then, would not have covered the barrister's actual performance in court). Having dismissed the complaint, his venom turned onto me. There was a considerable amount of 'how could an officer in the regiment behave like this?' and 'after 35 years in the army, what qualifies you to pass judgement… etc etc'. It then became even more personal. 'Are you a Freemason?' 'Are you homosexual?' and 'Are you bribed by barristers?' With that, I started to get a bit cross and wrote him a letter, which, when it inevitably reached the LSO, would have raised her eyebrows but I heard no more. Indeed, the LSO tended to be more supportive than critical on the majority of occasions. For instance I was glad she did not agree with the complainant who described me as 'deceptive and blatantly biased'. Although she did criticise me for failing to note that counsel had called a woman 'of limited intelligence'.

A rude and over-emotional Greek refused to accept counsel's advice. I'd dismissed the complaint some time ago but the Greek now threatened legal action against me for 'dismissing her [the defending counsel] as a witness'. He failed to understand counsel's role in court which I was careful to explain. Later, he telephoned my PA to threaten me. Being of a robust disposition, she sensibly did not put him through to me but referred him to

32. This immunity in court, in civil cases, was maintained and not changed until 20 July 2000 in the judgement in Arthur J S Hall & Co v. Simons.

the Chairman of the Bar, to whom, in theory anyway, I answered. I heard no more.

I don't suppose I should have been surprised but, from time to time, barristers had a go at me. They tended to be from the more inadequate level of quality and expertise. Dr A, astonishingly a member of the Bar, issued claims against me in the High Court for 'damages for breach of confidence, disclosure of source which leaked confidential information, and delivery up by defendant of all copies of information' – his words. He then produced particulars of claim against me. I passed the documentation to our in-house solicitors, who were bemused. He then tried to get at me directly by contacting the PCC. It was one of those cases in which if one did nothing it would evaporate of its own accord, which it duly did. Mr J, another barrister, tried to have me removed from investigating the complaint against him by appealing to the Chief Executive of the Bar, who refused. The man finally admitted to using a false name in his correspondence with us. Weird. A thoroughly unpleasant barrister – one of the few bad apples – demanded an apology from me for having the cheek to investigate a complaint against him. He didn't get it. Another thought it 'absurd' and 'infra dig' for me to seek evidence or ask her solicitors for it. I told her to read the Code of Conduct and get into the real world.

Sarcasm, pedantry, cynicism and pure name calling had their place. Mr C – he of innumerable faxes – asked if I merely signed someone else's draft? He did have a point since there were times when I rewrote a beautifully crafted opinion from a PCC member in my own, rather more basic, language. But I wasn't going to admit that. I had a not entirely unpleasant spat with a vexatious litigant. 'Quis custodiet ipsos custodes,'[33] he accusingly wrote to me. Clearly a classicist. I'd always rather fancied myself in the Praetorian Guard. Then Mr H claimed I had undeclared 'reasons' in the plural for not investigating his complaint. He was being pedantic. Any plural I used was merely that I had given him the 'reason' singular, three times. Mr T impugned

33. Who will guard the guards themselves? – Juvenal, Satire VI.

my honesty and integrity. Sadly, he was not the first to do so but no evidence – so far. Vitriol from Mr N. He threatened to come to London and beard me in my office. I don't think 'beard' was the word he actually used, but this is a story for sensitive readers. A complainant told me I had insulted him 'sarcastically'. He accused counsel of being 'on the take' and 'a fraud.' So he was not a stranger to sarcasm himself. An idiot from Australia called me a 'pea-brained pervert' which had a nice alliterative ring about it. Another called me a 'cretin'. LSO suggested reconsideration in this case. I refused and she dropped it. One I did like: a series of letters written to me by a certain Laura Norda. It took me some time to realise this was a sarcastic pseudonym.

There were threats, some mildly veiled but mostly blatant. A buffoon Iraqi barrister tried to take me to court. In Iraq? No thanks, even with business class and five star hotel. Then a first! I am accused of being biased, not against complainants, which is par for the course, but against gays. Whence the evidence? I was then threatened with racist proceedings against me for not finding evidence of racism by counsel, of which there was none. Nasty Mr Q threatened me again, this time with arrest, imprisonment and death, I think, but a little vague on detail. My old favourite, Mr B, threatened me with proceedings (for what?). I had dismissed his ninth complaint. Mr H accused me of being gay and bent. I told him I was neither, to his obvious disappointment. Iffy solicitors tried to have me removed for 'bias, ignorance and stupidity'. No joy – for them. Someone else threatened me with 'higher authority'. I don't think either of us knew what that entailed.

Some complainants wrapped their abuse in verbosity, quasi-legal language and incoherent English. A complainant demanded all the paperwork I had on him. I was very aware of the Freedom of Information Act and that anything I wrote could be disclosed, so not a problem. However, it would be wise to check with our solicitors first. Another complainant thought four years of depression and loss of sleep was a good reason for delay in making his complaint. However, he was well enough to complain to solicitors two years ago so why not me then? An abusive letter from Mr R followed, who was the boyfriend of Mrs M, protesting at my dismissal of her complaint. Both thoroughly nasty bits of work, led by him, a disbarred solicitor. The dotty Mrs T wrote again that I'm not interested in her complaint. I assure her I am but I'm awaiting counsel's clarification of her [inarticulate salvo] against courts, judges and the law in general. A complainant then instructed me to put his complaint to PCC while he complained about me to the chief executive. Clearly firing both barrels at once. A woman demanded to know my ethnic background and religion. I don't think either pleased her. Another woman accused me of 'aggression'. She should know, given the tone of her letters. Then venom from a complainant purely because she was black and I am white. A woman denied using words I attributed to her. She was wrong – I found them in her submission. She now says 'out of context'. This is, it appears, a new euphemism for lying. A complainant didn't like my dismissal and re-consideration, so told me to take a course in good manners. Likewise, chum. The ridiculous Mr & Mrs C sent 61 pages and 60 attachments to their complaint. Luckily this forest of paper was over three months from my earlier dismissal so out of time for submission to the LSO. I received, then, a cheeky email telling me the name of the member of the PCC to whom I should send the complaint. Full marks for knowing the system and trying to influence it. Not unnaturally the suggested member will, under no circumstances, see the complaint.

The know-alls tried to have me judicially reviewed. It is a complicated process, not for laymen. For example there was one against the LSO, me and counsel. Mr Justice Lightfoot dismissed it, with costs against the applicant, of £9,000. Not many tried that again.

All in a day's work. 'Clarity and transparency in the wider interests of justice,' the LSO would drily say.

However, I cannot leave this chapter without one of the more amusing stars of the complainant world, the famous 'Flying Vet,' Mr Maurice Kirk. He started with me in late 2001 with complaints against various barristers. Sadly, I have forgotten the detail, even if I really grasped it. I made contact with him and asked him if he could remember. His memory was as bad as mine but he did give me permission to publish his name 'as long as I told the truth'. There is considerable media cover of his escapades and brushes with the Law.[34]

Throughout one hearing his camper-van was parked outside the court, plastered with slogans including "Ever trusted a lawyer?" and "Corruption and conspiracy in our courts". I cannot say whether that is the 'truth' or not but readers can reach their own conclusions. He claimed he was once a drinking buddy of the late actor and hell raiser, Oliver Reed, and had in the past been convicted of air traffic offences when flying his private plane. (Did he fly under one of the London's Thames bridges? He wouldn't say but, secretly, I like to think he did). Famously, he was later arrested for landing a replica World War One biplane on private land near American President George W Bush's Texan ranch.

The bold Maurice was real character, who made the rest of complainants look very dreary. There was a touch of Colonel A D Wintle MC, The Royal Dragoons, about him.

Wintle, of course, was well before my time but, interestingly made legal history when he brought a legal action against a dishonest solicitor named Nye. He accused Nye of appropriating £44,000 (some £1,235,000 today) from the estate of Wintle's deceased cousin, by inveigling her into leaving the residue of her estate to Nye in her will. There was nothing in it for Wintle. To publicise the case, in 1955 Wintle served time in prison after forcing Nye to remove his trousers and submit to being photographed. He pursued Nye through the courts over the next three years, losing his case on two occasions. By 1958, Wintle ran out of money and had to present the case himself. On 26 November 1958, the Lords announced that they had found for Wintle. In its subsequent written reasons, the House of Lords held that the burden was on the solicitor Nye to establish that the gift of the

34. https://mauricejohnkirk.files.wordpress.com.
https://www.casemine.com/judgement/uk
https://www.penarthtimes.co.uk
https://mauricejohnkirk.com

residue of the deceased cousin's estate to the solicitor in the will that he had drawn was not the result of his fraud, and that he had failed to discharge this exceptionally heavy burden so that the trial jury's validation of the gift to Nye could not be allowed to stand. Wintle thus became the first non-lawyer to achieve a unanimous verdict in his favour in the House of Lords.

There is still a place for us non-lawyers.

I think both Kirk and Wintle would have enjoyed grappling with politicians - I didn't.

13
Political

ONCE A BARRISTER, ALWAYS a barrister, unless you are disbarred. You may not actually practise without continuing to keep up to date with professional qualifications and insurance. However, in the eyes of the public you are still, technically, a barrister and therefore a legitimate target for complaint. The fact that the grouse is against something that you have done is nothing to do with the practice of the law, is, to a complainant, irrelevant. Earlier, I explained how aggrieved divorcees sought to further their campaigns against spouses who happened to be barristers. When barristers become politicians or famous/infamous for activities not related to the legal profession, they can become a target. A few politicians managed to do both which could cause all sorts of problems.

A complainant's MP wrote to me enquiring in a self-important way 'whence delay?' The complainant, at no stage, had complained about delay. It was merely a typical point-scoring exercise by an MP no one had ever heard of, from an unknown constituency which you'd be pushed to find on a map, dying to squeeze one more vote. Another MP sent his constituent's complaint form, having completed it for him, which was a first for me. However, the complaint was so stale that it was impossible to investigate with any hope of a sensible outcome. Then there was a real madman: some sort of religious complaint against a well-known MP, who had been a barrister many years ago.

Someone complained against a current MP, who was a practising barrister, as the complainant had had no satisfaction in his political 'surgery'. So nothing to do with him being a barrister but a good try. He then went on to the LSO, Speaker of the House of Commons and Leader of the Opposition. A more interesting complaint came from the Belgrade Faculty of Law against a QC's role as *Amicus Curiae* at Milosevic's trial. Well above my pay grade and swiftly dismissed by the PCC.

Where barristers and politics really became entwined was over the Iraq War.

The Iraq War began in March 2003 when the US, joined by the UK, launched a "shock and awe" bombing campaign. Iraqi forces were quickly overwhelmed as coalition forces swept through the country. The Bush administration based its rationale for the war on the claim that Iraq had a weapons of mass destruction (WMD) programme, and that it posed a threat to the United States and its allies. No stockpiles of WMDs or an active WMD programme were ever found in Iraq. The reason for war faced heavy criticism both domestically and internationally.

Despite deep divisions within the Labour Party, in power at the time, and strong public opposition to a war with Iraq, it went ahead. When military inspectors failed to uncover weapons of mass destruction, the Blair government was accused of sexing up (sic) intelligence on which it had based its claim that Iraq was an imminent threat. There were a number of complaints against Blair, which I was able to dismiss on the basis that his actions as Prime Minister had nothing to do with his previous life as a barrister.

Not only was the Prime Minister, Tony Blair, a former barrister, but his wife, Cherie, was a practising one. The Attorney General, Lord Goldsmith, who advised the Prime Minister on the legality of going to war in Iraq, was also one. As such they were all targets of complainants who disapproved of the war and used the Bar Council's complaint system to further their campaigns.

MINDING THE LAW

Complaints against Lord Goldsmith, the Attorney General, were more difficult as he was, unlike the Prime Minister, a practising barrister. The nature of his legal advice to the government over the legality of the invasion was a significant political issue. The essence of complaints was that Goldsmith succumbed to political pressure to find legal justification for the use of force against Iraq. This, of course, was totally outside my customary run of complaints and was dragging me into a minefield of political controversy. The last thing I wanted was to be involved in this sort of thing. However, the rules were quite clear: a complaint against a barrister *had* to come through me initially, so I had no option but to deal with it.

The situation was, by any standards, complicated. In trying to unravel it, I had a serious off-the-record, lengthy meeting with a very senior Silk. Ultimately, I remitted it to the PCC. The complaints came from the former Overseas Development Secretary, Clare Short; a separate group of MPs; more than a dozen barristers (including four QCs); a journalist; and Reg Keys. Keys was a founder member of the campaign group Military Families Against the War. His son, Lance-Corporal Tom Keys, was one of six Royal Military Policemen killed by an Iraqi mob in Majar al-Kabir in June 2003. Mr Keys stood against Tony Blair at Sedgefield in the general election.[35] They accused Lord Goldsmith of breaching a section of the Bar's Code of Conduct which says a barrister must not 'permit his absolute independence, integrity and freedom from external pressures to be compromised', or 'compromise his professional standards in order to please his client, the court or a third party'.

The complaints were highly embarrassing because Lord Goldsmith was not only a former Chairman of the Bar but, as Attorney General, was also the titular head of the Bar. If found guilty, he could have been disbarred. A constitutional lawyer advised that the Bar Council had no jurisdiction in the matter as it had no power to investigate the provision of legal opinions to ministers by the government's law officers. Guided by the hand

35. Clare Dyer, Legal Editor, The Guardian 2 May 2005.

of a senior barrister, I drafted letters of dismissal to the complainants. A spokesman for Lord Goldsmith said he was 'very pleased' with the Bar Council's decision. 'He thinks it's come to the right conclusion. This is an attempt to involve the Bar Council in what is essentially a political dispute.'[36] He was right. Clare Short, not unnaturally, did not agree and published her correspondence with the Attorney General on her website. This named me and included the text of my dismissal letter. So much for the confidentiality of the complaints system.

Things were different with Lady Blair or Ms Cherie Booth QC as she liked to be called when working. She was, as a straightforward practising barrister, a much easier target. There were a number of complaints, effectively, having a go at her husband and nothing actually to do with her life as a barrister. I could dismiss these complaints, but with a certain amount of care.

The whole situation of barristers doing things other than legal matters or when their legal actions/advice raised questions of integrity, bias or jurisdiction caused headaches for the PCC and me, particularly the highly controversial Iraq War.

But what about the future?

36 *The Guardian* 14 July 2005.

14
The Future

L IKE ALL MAJOR INSTITUTIONS of State, it was proper that the legal profession's system should be subject to scrutiny and, if necessary, Parliamentary reform. The Bar was not to escape.

In 2003, Sir David Clementi[37] began a major review into the Regulatory Framework for Legal Services in England and Wales, with his recommendations published in December 2004. Clementi was tasked to consider what regulatory framework would best promote competition, innovation and the public and consumer interest in an efficient, effective and independent legal sector. Additionally, he was to recommend a framework which would be independent in representing the public and consumer interest, comprehensive, accountable, consistent, flexible, transparent, and no more restrictive or burdensome than is clearly justified.

There was considerable consultation in which I was marginally involved. On a first look, it had the threat which the Bar had strenuously resisted; government interference with the complaints system. However, it had to be said there was justification in that the government identified, believe it or not, some twenty-three individual providers of legal services. They included such persons

37 Sir David Clementi is a British business executive and a former Deputy Governor of the Bank of England. He was formerly the Chairman of the BBC.

as patent agents, licensed conveyancers, will-writers and trade-mark attorneys. Clearly this was a muddle and a minefield for laymen and users of legal services.

Not only did Clementi look at reforming the way the profession was regulated, he considered the fabric of the profession itself, specifically in relation to legal disciplinary and multi-disciplinary practices.[38] He concluded for reasons of independence, simplicity, consistency and flexibility, that a single independent complaints handling body for all consumer complaints was the best way forward. He maintained that this should be no more expensive than the current system and might be cheaper. He proposed that there should be an Office for Legal Complaints (OLC) to form part of the single Legal Services Board (LSB) framework, and would cover all front-line regulatory bodies covered by the LSB. Issues of professional conduct, including possible disciplinary action, would be handed down to front-line bodies. He accepted that, while there was case for dealing with such disciplinary matters in a uniform manner, with a simple disciplinary tribunal system, the existing disciplinary system worked reasonably well. It should, subject to only a few changes, be left broadly as it is. The LSB would be an independent legal services regulator accountable to Parliament. It would promote the interests of consumers and the public over the interests of legal services' providers. Clementi acknowledged that, rather than starting from scratch, the current system needed effective reform. Crucially, the LSB would be run by a majority of non-legally trained staff, while both its chairman and chief executive would come from non-legal backgrounds. The Law Society, Bar Council and other professional regulatory bodies would have to separate their regulatory and representative powers by creating the Solicitors Regulatory Authority (SRA) and the Bar Standards Board (BSB)). The Office for Legal Complaints would function under the supervision of the LSB. The Legal Services Ombudsman would be abolished.

38 These are where solicitors, barristers and/or legal executives set up together or where solicitors, other legal professionals, accountants or other non-legal professionals establish themselves as a group.

So would the Complaints Commissioner of the Bar but he was generous enough not to put that in writing.

After considerable experience at the leading edge of the complaints system, it was not surprising I had a number of views. The effect appeared to put the Bar back to where it was eight years ago when I started. The initiative the Bar adopted at the time (Independent Lay Commissioner, concept of Inadequate Professional Service, early diagnosis of complainant validity, conciliation and evidence subject only to the balance of probabilities) was to be subsumed by a central body, the OLC.

There were a number arguments arising from this which I took up with the Bar Council but before anyone thought I was trying to protect my own position, I was to retire, happily, just over a year later, so had nothing to lose except to preserve the very good work the Bar Council had done. Firstly, I was concerned that the OLC would be able to match the speed and quality of advice given by the senior practitioners of the PCC who gave their time for free. I understood the need for an overarching system to simplify, to what, for an outsider, was seen as a complex environment and to allay the fears that our complaints handling was not even-handed. At the same time, I could not help feeling that had it not been for the Law Society's difficulty in handling complaints against solicitors, we would not have reached this position. While I accepted it was difficult for Clementi to exclude the Bar from the overall solution, a better way was to capitalise on the success rate of the Bar's system, thereby retaining the goodwill of the barristers who work for nothing and those members of the Bar who financially contribute to it. The system could exist albeit under the umbrella of the OLC in a different format. I was concerned that the Bar was going to fall into the black hole of Government management about which many consumers are supremely critical. So stand by for Targets, Performance Standards, Manuals, Circulars, Protocols, Returns, Reports, Stakeholders and all the other impedimenta of officialdom.

There was, though, another view. The Bar could well be happy to be relieved of the responsibility for the complaints system.

THE FUTURE

No longer would they have the tiresome Complaints Commissioner on their backs, worrying them with statistics and exhorting them to do better. Nor would they have the *eminence grise* of the LSO in her lair in Manchester, threatening them with sanctions. They would be spared the running of a sophisticated and expensive assessment and referral system. The 'trade union' side of the Bar would be able to concentrate all its energies on supporting and defending it 'members' and challenging the OLC, without the constraint of having to see fair play for the other side. Worth consideration perhaps?

In the light of this review, it is worth quoting what the LSO had to say in her Report of the same year:

'I have found the Bar Council to work in a very open and co-operative manner. It has provided my office with a very thorough description of its complaint-handling operations and has actively invited our advice and comment regarding where and how it can make further improvements to those operations. Its approach has left my office with a strong impression that it is confident about its existing complaints-handling capabilities, but it is far from complacent and is constantly seeking to make improvements to its operations. The Bar Council's complaints service has clearly made good progress across a number of fronts during the past year and it appears to have very strong plans in place to continue to build on that progress during the year ahead.'

In accordance with the Clementi recommendations, the Legal Services Act 2007 established the Legal Services Board, under which the Office for Legal Complaints operated, which was responsible for the Legal Ombudsman's operations. The Act laid down, amongst others, the objectives for the legal regulators including the Bar Standards Board (BSB). On the face of it, this satisfied the Clementi aspiration to have complaints against lawyers, and others, handled centrally and independently from the providing institution. However, it didn't quite work like that.

If you want to complain against a barrister now, there are two ways of doing so. Assuming the barrister was acting for you, you approach the Legal Ombudsman on a matter of inadequate service (being rude, late, not listening to you etc). In this instance, the Legal Ombudsman can award compensation for this poor service, reduce fees or decide if you should receive an apology. However, the Ombudsman can only proceed after you have complained to the barrister's chambers, so you have to do that first, assuming you know which chambers the barrister operates from. If you get into a muddle and are unclear whether it is 'service' or 'misconduct', the Ombudsman will only deal with 'service' and refer your 'misconduct' complaint to the BSB. There is a distinct difference here compared to the old system. In my time you could complain about a barrister for anything and we would sort out whether it was a matter of inadequate professional service, to be dealt with by an Adjudication Panel, which I chaired, or misconduct which, if there was sufficient evidence, would be handled by a summary hearing or disciplinary tribunal. Now *you* have to choose.

If you are complaining about misconduct, you must establish the barrister has breached articles in the BSB handbook which contains the Code of Conduct. Not something you have by your bedside at night, I'd suggest. When a complaint is received from you or referred by the Legal Ombudsman for allegation of misconduct, it is forwarded to the Contact and Assessment Team to decide what action is needed. If it is decided a formal investigation is required, the case is then passed to the Investigations and Enforcement Team. Once all the information has been gathered, the team looks at whether there is enough evidence that the rules have been broken and the risk [their word] is high enough for enforcement action to be taken. The Investigations and Enforcement Team has the power to decide to take no action, issue a written warning or institute a fine up to £1,000 for an individual barrister. They are the permanent staff of the BSB and, if they require technical legal advice, they instruct a barrister, who is paid. This is completely different to the PCC whose members operated for free. The Legal and Enforcement department also deals with concerns about barristers' fitness to practise for health reasons, and with interim suspensions from practice pending conclusion of disciplinary proceedings where the alleged misconduct poses a serious risk to the public.[39] If the Investigations and Enforcement Team does not have the power to decide the outcome of a case, it is passed to a five-person panel of the Independent Decision-making Body to make a decision. All decisions to refer cases to disciplinary action would be taken by this panel. The five members are drawn from a larger group but must include three laymen and two barristers. They would assess whether there was enough evidence to show that the barrister had not followed the rules and decide what action to take, if any. They might decide to impose an administrative sanction or, if the issue is more serious, they could pass it on to a disciplinary tribunal or to the determination by 'consent' procedure for a decision on whether the barrister has committed professional misconduct. I am a little vague as to exactly what 'consent' means here. Serious cases of misconduct are heard by disciplinary tribunals. Sanctions may include a fine of up to £50,000 or a period of suspension. In the most serious cases, the tribunal may decide to disbar the barrister. The disciplinary tribunal cannot award compensation.

A parallel function is provided by the independent reviewer. The Reviewer's role is to assist in ensuring that the regulatory decisions remain of a high quality, effective and fair, and that all the correct processes and procedures have been followed properly. This is not a substitute for the Legal Service Ombudsman to whom you could appeal under the previous arrangements. If you do not like what has happened, you have no recourse other than judicial eview. In my time the LSO played a very important role as the last resort for the complainant and the checks and balances on what we did.

Looking carefully at it, there seems to be little real difference to what I and the PCC did but with more bureaucratic layers and barristers' opinions paid for. The inadequate service element has been completely removed from the Bar and put to the legal ombudsman. The Bar is still, effectively, dealing with barrister's misconduct and disciplining the barrister where appropriate. The impression I get is that complaints are handled much more clini-

39 BSB annual report 2020/2021

cally, less interaction with the complainant and more emphasis on correcting the barrister's performance with the aim of reducing 'risk' to the public. It has become more corporate and less personal. What about the results of this new arrangement by 2022?

According to an analysis by *The Times*, the legal ombudsman has the second-worst record of all the ombudsman services on TrustPilot, the reviews website. Of the 185 reviews listed for the Legal Ombudsman, 178 give only one star, meaning it has an average rating of 1.2 out of 5. Only the parliamentary and health service ombudsman has a worse record with an average rating of 1.1. In total nearly 6,000 cases are waiting to be investigated, more than double the number two years ago.[40] So, don't bother.

The BSB is thin on statistics in its report of 2020/21. It merely lists '1,898 new reports about barristers' (1,477 in 2019/20), of which 20 barristers had a disciplinary finding against them, nine were suspended and four disbarred. Presumably 'new reports' is a euphemism for complaints. To put it into context, over a five year period in my time, the average number of complaints per year was 700. In my annual reports I analysed the origins of complaints, what happened to them, the LSO's statistics and the specific outcome of Adjudication Panels.

In March 2006, I was released for good behaviour, after nine years, to be succeeded by a civil servant from the Lord Chancellor's office and the institution of the Bar Standards Board. I think the Bar Council could see the heavy bureaucratic hand of government and decided to have an 'insider' to handle change rather than a complete layman such as me. I suspect that, by doing so, they lost the personal touch, which I reckoned to be an essential part of the process. Ordinary members of the public often found the language and behaviour of barristers arcane and difficult to understand. While they may have been dissatisfied with my ultimate decision, at least I was 'one of them', not a lawyer and could, hopefully, explain the intricacies of the legal world. My main drive was to be fair and principled in my dealings with them and the barristers.

---

40 'Legal complaints go untouched for years' Andrew Ellson, Consumer Affairs Correspondent, *The Times* 30 July 2022.

THE FUTURE

Overall I enjoyed my time. It had its moments – the graffiti-spraying, the thirty pieces of silver and the tin of Argentinean corned beef, to say nothing of my appearance for contempt in the High Court. From a strictly personal point of view I like to think it was a success. Here was I, a seasoned army officer, but with absolutely no experience of the world of civilian life, at age 56, launching into something entirely new. Not only was it new to me but also to the Bar which had never had a complaints commissioner before: a risk to us both. However, I was taking up employment within a highly disciplined organisation. I had the support of an outstanding PA, highly competent executive secretaries and in-house solicitors, all of whom remained with me for the whole of my time. They were my trusted colleagues and confidants, rather like I'd had in the army. Overall, I had the encouragement, confidence and backing of the Bar Council.

A number of my contemporaries, on retirement, worked for security companies, particularly if they had Special Forces backgrounds; some joined the charitable sector and some merely sailed their yachts or improved their golf handicap. Mine was not a soft option; I worked a full day, five days a week and, bearing in mind, *every* complaint had to go through me, you can imagine the depth of files in my in-tray on return from holiday. What did I gain over my nine years? I think I proved you *can* have a 'second life' and there is a valuable, and satisfying, contribution that older people can make to society.

At my final appearance before the assembled Bar Council, Stephen Hockman QC, the chairman made the following kind remarks;

'Mr Scott has made an outstanding contribution to the work of the Bar Council over the last nine years. His wise approach to complaints has been one of the crucial factors in the success of the Bar's system. The fact that the overwhelming majority of his decisions are endorsed by the independent LSO, while at the same time keeping the confidence of the Bar itself, shows that he has managed to tread a difficult tightrope with skill and aplomb. His commitment, resilience and integrity have been crucial to what have been an outstandingly successful nine years. We will miss him greatly and wish him a very long and happy retirement'.

Just in case you are ever in the unfortunate position of having to complain against a barrister, you might like to make use of one or two of the following little jewels which I collected over my time:

1. By retaining this barrister at the Bar, we will be depriving an English village of its idiot.

2. Mr X QC has a difficulty for every solution.

3. This barrister is so cold-blooded that if a mosquito bit him it would die of pneumonia.

4. If this barrister were to swim through shark infested water he would survive, thanks to professional courtesy.

5. Barristers like Mr X do not grow on trees, they hang from them.

6. A suitable finishing touch to this barrister's opinion would be a Swan Vestas match.

7. He would be out of his depth in a car park puddle.

8. This man is a phoney; even the wool he pulls over your eyes is 50% polyester.

9. This young barrister could give failure a bad name.

But my favourite: He will not set the Thames on fire but if you want it done he'll know who can do so and where the matches are.

Happy days.